1977

This ____ ___y be kept

PERSONAL COMMUNICATION
IN HUMAN RELATIONS

GAYLORD 1·

sTudiEs of ThE pERsoN

This Studies of the Person Series was founded and developed by Carl R. Rogers and William R. Coulson, and is now under the managing editorship of William R. Coulson.

PERSONAL COMMUNICATION
IN HUMAN RELATIONS

kim Giffin
The University of Kansas

bobby R. PATTON
The University of Kansas

Charles E. Merrill Publishing Company
A Bell & Howell Company
Columbus, Ohio

Published by
Charles E. Merrill Publishing Company
A Bell & Howell Company
Columbus, Ohio 43216

Library of Congress Catalog Card Number: 73–92001

ISBN: 0–675–08819–4

1 2 3 4 5 6 / 78 77 76 75 74

Printed in the United States of America

Dedicated to our best friends:

Eddina
Bonnie
Kitty and Charles
Fritz
and Spike

CONTENTS

pReFACE

Human relations is a broad and ambiguous concept. People relate to one another in many ways. Their interactions include such things as talking together, giving one another physical assistance, instructing or helping each other, and engaging in mutual sexual gratifications. Almost any behavior on the part of one person may be viewed as a way of relating to some other person.

Our interest in this book is focused primarily upon human interaction in the form of communication. We have chosen as our primary concern the ways in which people relate to one another in the act of talking. We recognize that such communicative actions include both verbal and nonverbal behavior. We also understand that how we are perceived influences the meaning ascribed to our communication acts. Further, we recognize that this ascribed meaning includes educated guesses regarding our motives for engaging in interaction. All of these concerns are included in our concept of communication.

"Personal communication" is taken to be expressions of the "self" —indicating a desire and willingness to share feelings, perceptions, and ideas, particularly as they relate to me, to you, and to our relation-

Preface

ship. For our colleagues in the professional discipline of human communication, this book constitutes a statement of philosophy—a summary of concerns and commitments that such professional people can make to the broader human potential movement.

Our context has been the classroom laboratory group operating as a T-Group. Typically, in such an experience, from ten to twenty individuals face the task of creating, developing, and maintaining a small social organization—a miniature society—within a relatively short but concentrated period of time. This emerging social organization faces real, hard problems of social formation, individual relationships, and work achievement. Although the T-Group is a miniature society, it has aspects not typically found in social organizations. Peculiar to the T-group is its process of inquiry, experimentation, and exploration into its own activities. Peculiar, at least for the most part, is its sole purpose of helping individual members to learn; the process of developing a group in which to learn becomes the means for achieving personal growth.

While the T-group and its task are unique, they are not artificial. The group in its beginning has blurred or ambiguous fundamental ingredients of social organizations, such as authority and power structure, processes of goal formation, norms of personal and group behavior, procedures for productive work, and expectations for leader and member behavior. These ambiguities must be reduced through the hard work of the group's members. Their efforts at establishing relationships and solving problems provide the communication behaviors that can in turn provide the bases for personal learning.

We are indebted to our students and colleagues for their insightful advice and comments as the manuscript was developing. In addition we want to thank the following for their help in typing the manuscript: Marilyn Blubaugh, Lynn Goodnight, Mona Hargadine, and Susan Harshaw.

1

laboratory groups in education

Utter frustration—disorganization; uninstructive, disappointing. Unpleasurable experience; stultifying—unstimulating.[1]

Most significant and helpful in facilitating a better understanding of myself and my relationship with others.[2]

It's too bad you're not a "self-actualizing" person, Charlie Brown. Self-actualizing persons are free from fears and inhibitions. They accept themselves and they accept others. . . . They have self-esteem and confidence.

Can I become a self-actualizing person?

No way! Five cents, please.[3]

Educators have always been concerned about the most effective and efficient means of dispensing knowledge. The earliest assumptions are still explicit in the semantics of the education profession. I am the "teacher" possessing the knowledge and the expertise to dispense it in such a fashion that learning will take place. You are the "student" coming to me because of your desire and motivation to learn what I have to offer.

1

Methods of instruction have varied from the inductive approach to learning reflected in the Socratic dialogues to the deductive prescriptions of the early sophists. More recently we have introduced new terms and concepts that add alternatives to instruction, but also lend confusion as to counter-philosophies of teaching: behavioral objectives, programmed learning, mass-lectures, humanistic teaching, pre-schools, behaviorism, operant conditioning, affective learning. During the sixties and seventies there has been a growing interest in approaches to learning that assign to the emotional factor in education a role on the same level as the traditional substantive content and skills.

Terms such as "laboratory training," "sensitivity training," and "human relations" may have imprecise connotations, but they are used with such frequency today, and have inspired such controversy, that objective discussion is difficult. Yet as Max Birnbaum has stated:

> By whatever name it is known, however, human relations training is capable, if properly employed, of producing substantial educational change. It holds tremendous potential for improving education by dealing with its affective components, reducing the unnecessary friction between generations, and creating a revolution in instruction by helping teachers to learn how to use the classroom group for learning purposes.[4]

Let us look at this educational phenomenon in greater detail.

LABORATORY TRAINING

Characteristics

Several authors have attempted to describe laboratory training, and to distinguish it from therapy on the one hand, and conventional education on the other. Egan, notably concerned with the psychological aspects of training, has listed these characteristics:

1. Learning through actual experience in small groups.
2. A climate of experimentation.
3. A group size "small enough to allow each participant the opportunity to contribute to the interaction of the group," but "large enough to allow the participants to space their contributions" based on the demands of the group and the individual's needs and capabilities.
4. Feedback.
5. Leadership in the form of a trainer or facilitator.

6. Dealing with emotions and their effects on the communication processes.
7. Support, or "security measures," to match the demanded anxiety-arousing behavior.
8. Ambiguity (although this may be mitigated when it is counter to the laboratory goals).
9. Exercises.
10. Participants drawn from normal rather than psychiatric populations.[5]

Gibb stressed even more clearly the distinction between training and therapy by noting that laboratory training focuses on the "here and now," and deals with the available interpersonal experiences within the group, studies group processes and actions between members, provides the opportunity for members to try new behaviors, and seeks for members seen by themselves and the trainer as normal to experience personal growth. *Not* normally characteristic of laboratory training would be primary interest in historical information which members might bring to the group from their organizations or families, analysis of unconscious motivations which may lie behind experiences in the group, the study of leader-member relationships, new insight or motivation, or participants drawn from other than normal populations.[6] Many of the same characteristics of laboratory training, especially its experiential focus, help distinguish it from forms of traditional education as well.[7]

Varieties

Laboratory training has been described as:

a variety of small group experiences which range from intensive, emotionally cathartic, personalized encounter groups to highly skill-oriented leadership and team development programs and including groups focusing on sensitivity to others, personal growth, helping others, conflict resolution, community action, racial relations, and executive development.[8]

Rogers briefly described and named a number of laboratory training groups. Several of them are closely related and are grouped together to outline two forms of training which are of special interest in this study. The first grouping is the T-group, encounter group, and sensitivity training group. Rogers described the T-group as originally focusing on the development of human relations skills, but recognized that the title has more recently been applied to a wider range of laboratory experiences. The encounter group he described as an experiential process for personal growth and the improvement of interpersonal communication. He considered sensitivity training a term commonly used to refer to either the T-group or encounter group.[9] Gibb also equated sensitivity training with the T-group, but distinguished such training from the encounter group, which he described as "therapy for normals" focusing primarily on the openness of communcation of a person with himself and others.[10] Thomas highlighted the similarities and differences between the encounter group and the T-group. Both, he wrote, are frequently composed of eight to fifteen members, relatively unstructured, interested in the "here and now," and employ feedback of members to each other to develop new images and behaviors. The primary interest of the T-group, as defined by Thomas, is the group, and members learn about the group process by building their own. The trainer serves as an ideal, but reserved, group member. Thomas described the encounter group trainer as more active and directive, leading the group in revealing the inner self, and assisting in the pursuit of personal growth. This form of training would often be the most intense and personally involving of the two types of groups. Another distinction made by Thomas was that the T-group is conducted largely on the verbal level, while the encounter group also deals with the nonverbal elements of human communication.[11] Another position has been expressed in the catalog for the Midwest Center for Human Potential: encounter groups were known "in olden days" as T-groups or sensitivity training.[12]

The second grouping of Rogers' varieties of laboratory training includes organizational development, team building, and task-oriented groups.[13] The last variety Rogers identified as focusing on the interpersonal elements involved in the tasks of a group, and widely used in industry. The other varieties he described as useful in developing leadership skills, and the formation of close and effective working groups.[14] These varieties of training have become common elements of a program known as organization development. These two major forms of laboratory training are not mutually exclusive, however. Their relationship is suggested in this description of sensitivity training by Egan:

... a particular kind of laboratory training in which personal and interpersonal issues are the direct focus of the group. Other goals, such as learning about group processes and developing skills for diagnosing group and organizational behavior, are not eliminated, but they are incidental and therefore subordinated to the goal of dealing with personal and interpersonal deficiencies and potentialities.[15]

Rogers suggested that organization development "does not differ greatly from the personal development which is the goal of most encounter groups."[16]

Our major concern is with laboratory groups in which no task is assigned other than to learn about ourselves from other members of the group.

Hypothesis and Assumptions

Rogers has proposed a set of "practical hypotheses" that attempt to explain the subtle processes within a laboratory training group. They are:

A facilitator can develop, in a group which meets intensively, a psychological climate of safety in which freedom of expression and reduction of defensiveness gradually occur.

In such a psychological climate many of the immediate feeling reactions of each member toward others, and of each member toward himself, tend to be expressed.

A climate of mutual trust develops out of this mutual freedom to express real feelings, positive and negative. Each member moves toward greater acceptance of his total being—emotional, intellectual, and physical—as it *is*, including its potential.

With individuals less inhibited by defensive rigidity, the possibility of change in personal attitudes and behavior, in professional methods, in administrative procedures and relationships, becomes less threatening.

With the reduction of defensive rigidity, individuals can hear each other, can learn from each other, to a greater extent.

There is the development of feedback from one person to another, such that each individual learns how he appears to others and what impact he has in interpersonal relationships.

With this greater freedom and improved communication, new ideas, new concepts, new directions emerge. Innovations can become a desirable rather than a threatening possibility.

These learnings in the group experience tend to carry over, temporarily or more permanently, into the relationships with spouse, children, students, subordinates, peers, and even superiors following the group experience.[17]

Campbell and Dunnette, after examination of a number of cases of laboratory training, summarized what appeared to them to be the assumptions, although not always explicitly stated, which lay behind the training. One was that lack of interpersonal competence is a universal malady, shown in distorted self-images, faulty perceptions of others, and poor communication skills. The other assumptions dealt with the behavior of interpersonally incompetent persons assembled in laboratory training groups, and the effects of their behavior. The remaining assumptions were:

1. In-group behavior will be typical of participants' behavior.
2. Psychological safety will develop within hours of the formation of the group.
3. "A substantial number of group members, when confronted with others' behaviors and feelings in an atmosphere of psychological safety, can produce articulate and constructive feedback."
4. Participants can agree on an exhibited behavior.
5. Feedback will be relatively complete and will deal with significant aspects of the interactions of the group members.
6. Anxiety facilitates new learning.
7. Learnings from the group experience will be transferred to the members' normal environments.[18]

Objectives

The assumption of a universal need for improved personal competence also suggests the tone of the objectives for laboratory training. Gibb has computed the six most commonly stated objectives of training, as he found them in the literature. One is to increase the participant's sensitivity, expressed variously as spontaneity, tolerance of new information, and an awareness of the feelings and perceptions of others. Closely related to this are two other common objectives— functional attitudes toward others, and interdependent behavior. The former would be shown through reduced prejudice and authoritarianism and a greater acceptance of others; and the latter, through support for democratic leadership, teamwork, and increased task effectiveness.[19]

The remaining three common objectives, as Gibb found them in the literature, are managing feelings, managing motivations, and acquiring functional attitudes toward self. The first of these refers to the capacity for expressing feelings, and increased owning of them, as well as congruity between feelings and actual behavior. Management of motivations would be shown in self-actualization, and greater energy level. Acquiring functional attitudes toward self would result in greater confidence, self-acceptance, and self-esteem, and in congruity of self-image and ideals.[20]

Effects and Problems

A number of researchers have attempted to evaluate how well laboratory training has met the stated objectives, and the validity of the assumptions and hypotheses. Gibb, after a survey of research on each of the objectives of laboratory training, each type of laboratory group, and selected other factors, such as group composition, duration, and leader behavior, concluded that the results were "certainly controversial and open to legitimate multiple interpretations." Nevertheless, he felt personally convinced that changes were produced in sensitivity, feeling management, directionality of motivation, attitudes toward self and others, and interdependence.[21] Campbell and Dunnette were likewise cautious. They found the evidence, though limited, convincing that T-group training did induce behavioral changes in "back home" settings. In another area, they were less convinced:

It still cannot be said with any certainty whether T groups lead to greater or lesser changes in self-perceptions than other types of group experience, the simple passage of time, or the mere act of filling out a self-description questionnaire.[22]

Another study of the effects of laboratory groups also indicated some evidence of changes, but not overwhelming evidence. Cooper and Mangham found that observers generally agreed that persons who have attended T-groups show improved skills in diagnosing individual and group behavior, more tolerance and consideration, clearer communication, and "greater action skill" and flexibility; and that the changes lasted "for some time after training, though there are conflicting reports of fade-out after 10-12 months."

Schein and Bennis have stressed the need for strictly voluntary attendance for laboratory training. They have indicated that not only is learning unlikely under forced participation, but it is unethical for an organization to influence interpersonal behavior. They noted that insistence on voluntary attendance often resulted in a situation where those who need the training the most refuse to attend, and those who need it least attend readily. To overcome this problem, they suggested that pressures be avoided, even in organizations using a massive training program, but that individuals be given adequate orientations to enable them to make "meaningful" choices.[23]

A final problem with laboratory training to be considered here is image. Schein and Bennis comment that organizational laboratory training is in no way intended to "make people happy" or to assist organizations in manipulation of personnel. Common images of laboratory training persist, however. The laboratory group is seriously classified as a "fashionable therapy"—along with drugs and sex.[24] Sensitivity training has been portrayed in jest as a fad response to the excessive use of deodorants.[25] Spectacular exposés appear, as in a recent series in a Chicago newspaper. An introduction to the series began, " 'One out of 10 persons who joins an encounter group is liable to become a casualty,' charges psychologist and psychotherapist Bruce Maliver." While such charges lack definitive verification, they do create an image problem for educators who might otherwise seek to employ laboratory training approaches to learning.

"SENSITIVITY EDUCATION"[26]

Educational psychologists have told us that learning consists of two factors: exposure to new experience or learning, and the discovery of personal meaning for the learner. Educators have long been concerned with providing the information; the primary weaknesses in our system are in the lack of personal meanings provided.

In many classrooms attempts are made to create a climate that encourages students to report and discuss the ways they are feeling about themselves, one another, and the teachers. Yet opinions surveyed and reported in the March 1970 issue of *Nation's Schools* indicated that educators are largely on the fence about laboratory training. Uncertainty about the preparation of teachers and insufficient and conflicting information on the effects of intensive group experiences were the principal reasons given by school administrators for suspending judgment. The prevailing attitude seemed to be one of "wait and see."

PERSONAL LEARNING IN LABORATORY GROUPS

The procedure for learning about and improving one's ability to relate with others appears to be based upon three elements:

1. *Learning by Experiencing Behavior, Including Emotions.* Students become more aware and sensitive to their own needs and feelings as well as those of others in the group.

2. *Learning by the Inductive Process.* Instead of hearing stated principles and then hoping for an opportunity to see or experience them in a real-life setting, the student will see and experience personal behaviors in the group. The student will be able to compare his perceptions and experiences with those of other group members. Eventually, personal statements of general principles of human relations will be derived. Hopefully, reading this book may contribute to this process; you the reader, however, are encouraged to test statements made in this book against your personal experiences and that of other group members.

3. *Learning to Handle Ambiguous Situations.* A student's observations will often be somewhat different from those of others in the same situation; this resultant ambiguity can be distressing. Learning along with others in a laboratory group can help the student to see the causes of this ambiguity and thus to tolerate it when necessary. The means of education—growth and change—is through *personal communication*—expressions of "self." We learn as we share feelings, perceptions, and ideas, particularly as they relate to me, to you, and to our relationship. We are thus concerned with the nature of human relationships and the significant contributions that personal communication makes.

In the next chapter we shall explore the role that personal communication plays in the development of self.

2

pERSONAL COMMUNiCATiON:
THE dEvElOpMENT Of SElf

Communication is a difficult term to conceptualize.[1] We have pur-
posely narrowed our concern in this book to communication that
characterizes effective interaction in laboratory groups—the individual's personal communication. In seeking a manageable definition of
personal communication, we hypothesize that it is related to: (a)
degree of openness, (b) feelings and perceptions, (c) "here and now"
statements, and (d) degree of specificity. Thus, we suggest that personal communication is the offering of *personal* (owned) *information*
(feelings and/or perceptions) about *events* (actions, behaviors, expressions) which are mutually *relevant* (related) to the "here and
now" in an *unambiguous* manner. The underlying factor in this
definition is the degree of openness. The extent to which information
in interactive situations is given openly is indicative of the degree
that the interaction is truly personal communication. We shall examine this concept of openness in our personal communication and
then the role that this process plays in the development of our self-
concepts.

OPENNESS IN PERSONAL COMMUNICATION[2]

Much of the research done on openness might be more appropriately referred to as research on self-disclosure or revealingness. The concepts studied suggest primarily a personal dimension of expression (self-disclosure) or openmindedness (receptivity of information). Rokeach, in his studies of dogmatism, has presented a conceptualization of openness which is often used in studies concerned with individuals in group interaction situations.[3] He has presented a formulation of "openmindedness" or openness related to receptivity rather than openness of expression, the highly valued construct in maintenance groups. Jourard, in his work on self-disclosure, has focused on the types of information people are willing to share with others.[4] It is Jourard's basic premise that individuals who are able to be relatively transparent are more healthy emotionally, and are more receptive to growth experiences. A question arises as to whether the self-disclosing of information to others is, in and of itself, increasing transparency or is reflective of open behavior. For example, the norms of certain groups dictate the nature of the self-disclosure. Some groups demand disclosure by their members on the nature of sexual behaviors. The participant might well disclose extensive information about his behaviors without revealing honestly or openly his feeling about them, his feeling about himself or equally important, discussing the nature of his feelings while engaging in such disclosure. These conceptions of openness do not seem to be in line with the concept of openness discussed in the T-group or laboratory group setting, although they may be related. Our view of openness suggests an emphasis on openness of expression rather than openmindedness in Rokeach's use of the term. It more closely reflects Jourard's notions of self-disclosure or transparency.

Jourard advances the thesis that accurate portrayal of the self to others is an identifying criterion of healthy personality, and that it is the basis of establishing close, interpersonal relationships, while neurosis is related to an inability to know one's real self and to make it known to others. Fromm, Riesman, and Horney have dealt with the tendency among persons in our society to misrepresent the self to others, e.g. the "other-directed character," the "marketing personality," and the "self-alienated" individual.

From our perspective, openness and self-disclosure are so entwined with personal communication that they are virtually synonymous. Personal communication refers to the extent to which it is owned information, probably reflected by the use of such words as

"I feel," "my perception," etc. It would seem that the movement from general ownership, "People usually think . . ." to more specific ownership such as "I think . . ." reflects an increase in ownership, consequently an increase in the level of openness. (It has been noted that statements of feeling or perception might be owned but not be accurate reflections of what or how one actually perceives or feels. It is suggested that this then is a question of honesty. This concept of openness might be helpful in defining "honesty" in interpersonal relations more operationally.)

Specifying the source of the feeling or perception seems supportive to our concept of openness. Saying, "John, I feel . . . ," is less ambiguous than saying, "Some people in here make me feel . . . ," and even less ambiguous than saying, "People who . . . (do such and such) . . . make me feel . . .". Identifying the source, John, is important in that it reduces ambiguity and requires that the speaker be open about the source of his feelings.

Many of the feelings or perceptions people have of others come as a result of specific observed behaviors. It seems that openness is enhanced when the specific behaviors leading to a feeling or perception are stated. To say, "John, I am angry about your aggressiveness, like when you just took over and told Sue what to do," gives John clearer data about himself and the way he is in the group. To say, "John, I get angry when you are aggressive," gives him only a peek at the things he does which contribute to the perceptions others have of him.

It might also be argued that indication of attached causal relationships between perceptions would be supportive to optimum openness. For instance, "John, you are so aggressive, I think it's because you feel insecure in the group," expresses not only the observable behavior which created the perception but perceives further the cause of that overt behavior.

Events are those experiences which stimulate the formulation of feelings or perceptions. They may vary widely in nature, dimension, and content. A mutual relevance of events suggests that those events stimulating perception should be couched in the "here and now" of the interaction. Events which occurred long ago between persons have impact on the nature of present perceptions and feelings. Data generated by such "there and then" events is open to the extent it is related to the present feelings and perceptions of the interactors.

Finally, such expressions must be made in unambiguous ways. It is assumed that behavior which is ambiguous, intentionally ambiguous, is defensive or potentially defensive. The greater latitude one has for reinterpreting his expression (i.e. the more ambiguous he is) the less committed he is to the open expression of presently existing feelings and perceptions.

After considerable deliberation about whether these ingredients of openness are additive, how they are weighted, and whether they represent a complete listing of the components of an openness paradigm, it was decided that they might be arranged to present a profile of openness. The schema shown in table 1 was developed to represent this arrangement.

Briefly described, this schema represents eight factors seen as supportive to the optimum of openness in personal communication. They are presented as continua because the delineation of specified amounts or degrees of these factors is not known. It is possible, however, to speculate on such degrees. The following examples will consider, in turn, each of eight factors, varying one of the factors along the conceptualized continuum while holding the other seven factors constant.

Mutually Relevant, "Here and Now"

Example 1. "Don, I feel very hostile toward you right now; whenever I expressed a thought, verbally, to the group, you reacted to me in a negative way."

This statement is (1) here and now, (2) expresses an owned feeling toward a specified source, (3) identifies a behavior (reaction to me), and (4) expresses a perception of that behavior ("negative way").

Example 2. "Don, I feel hostile toward you at times, like whenever I express a thought, verbally, to the group—you always react to me in a negative way."

Note the shift from the immediate here and now to expression of feelings which only occur at times and which are, possibly, not active at the moment. This shift is important because processing of the feelings is based on recall over time as opposed to evaluation of the feelings while they are fresh or occurring.

Example 3. "Don, I didn't like you very well back when we were in high school; you and your friends used to really put people down all the time."

The shift is now completely away from the "now" experience. In fact, the speaker would probably deny existence of such feelings at this

Table 1

Openness in Personal Communication: THEORETIC PROFILE

Mutually Relevant	Here and now: feelings expressed are current and based on immediate interactions	Here, not now: feelings expressed relate to immediate interaction but are not current	Not here, not now: feelings expressed are not current and relate to past experience unrelated to present interaction	*Not Mutually Relevant*
Feeling Owned	Owned: Use of "I feel"	General ownership: "Some of us feel" Other owned: "Some people"	General Other: "People . . ." or "Society . . ."	*Not Owned Feeling*
Source of Feeling Specified	Directly specified: "John, toward you I . . ."	Indirectly specified: "Some people make me feel . . ."	Generally specified: "I feel around people (in general)"	*Source Not Specified*
Causal Connection (Re: Feeling)	Stated: "because . . ."	Suggested: "may be because"	Alluded to: "there may be a reason"	*No Causal Connection*
Perception Owned	Owned: "I think . . ."	General ownership: "Some of us think . . ." Other owned: "Some people think . . ."	General other: "People, Society"	*Perception Not Owned*
Source of Perception Specified	Directly specified: "Mary, you . . ."	Indirectly specified: "Some people in the group '. . ."	Generally specified: "I think people are usually . . ."	*Source of Perception Not Specified*
Causal Connection (Re: Perception)	Stated: "You're aggressive because you're insecure . . ."	Suggested: "The reason may be that you're insecure . . ."	Alluded to: "There may be a reason . . ."	*No Causal Connection*
Behavior Specified	Specific behavior cited: ". . . you're yelling at Sue . . ."	Type of behavior specified: ". . . say unkind things"	Existence of behaviors indicated but not cited: ". . . some of the things you do . . ."	*No Behavior Specified*

15

point in the relationship. Whether these feelings are part of the experience "here" is also subject to question. The speaker might indicate that those feelings occurred outside of this experience entirely, such as "at work," "when we were younger," etc., and that they never were part of the experience in this group interaction.

Example 4. "Don, I was warned to be wary of you; I heard you had a reputation for responding negatively to the things people said."

In this example, the speaker has still owned the feeling but it did not occur in the here or the now of the relationship. It is possible that this feedback is mutually relevant in that it has effect on the speaker's behavior in the presence of Don, but its relevance could easily be denied.

Feelings, Owned

Example 1. "Jane, I think you are too authoritative in the group and lead too much. It makes me very uncomfortable and I don't feel able to comment, or make suggestions after you speak."

This example, as example 1 above, includes the most open aspects of all factors in the paradigm. We can, however, vary the *owned* factor in this statement.

Example 2. "Jane, some of us think you are too authoritative in the group and lead too much. We're uncomfortable."

The ownership is now collective rather than individual. Jane may not know whether to include the speaker in the group or not.

Example 3. "Jane, some people in the group think . . ."

Ownership has shifted from a collective to other owned. "Some people in the group" now own the feeling and that might easily exclude the speaker.

Example 4. "Jane, the group thinks . . ."

In this example, ownership is in a general other, "the group," and may not be found in any individual. Here the speaker has protected not only himself but all of the other group members as well. If the speaker were to say, "Jane, you are too authoritative and people don't comment after you speak," he would be offering a perception but no feeling.

Feelings, Source Specified

Example 1. (Using example 1 above, the source is specified. The feelings of the speaker are caused by Jane, whose behavior —speaking—is too authoritative. It might be possible to provide this feedback without being specific as to source.)

Example 2. "Some people in this group are too authoritative and lead too much, it makes me very uncomfortable and I don't feel able to comment or make suggestions after they speak."

The shift here is from Jane to "some people." Openness in the fullest degree might follow only after assurance that the speaker should disclose the names of those people who make him feel that way.

Example 3. "Some people are too authoritative and lead too much. I feel uncomfortable and don't feel able to comment or make suggestions after they speak."

Some people, not necessarily in this group, create these feelings in the speaker. The data provided to others are still more general and less usable to them in dealing with the feelings of the speaker in this group situation.

Perception, Owned

Perception of others may enhance the openness paradigm in many instances. The dynamics of this factor are very similar to those of the feeling factor.

Example 1. "John, although I know practically nothing about you, I feel good about you; I think you are sad and withdrawn, unwilling to tell what you feel."

The speaker expresses his feeling and perception of John. He indicates that it is his perception.

Example 2. "John, although we know practically nothing about you, I feel good about you; some people say you seem sad and withdrawn, unwilling to tell what you feel."

In this example, the perception is attributed to others. The speaker is free to say "Of course, I don't see you that way ...."

Example 3. "John, we know little about you, you haven't said much; people usually figure quiet people to be sad or withdrawn."

In this example, the perception is owned by some generalized way people are, not by the speaker.

Example 4. "**John, I feel good about you in this group.**" No perception is offered to John, but for reasons not stated the speaker feels good about him.

Perception, Source Specified

Example 1. (**Example 1 above, under Perception, owned, specifies the source. It is possible to consider that example with the source not specified or specified generally.**)

Example 2. "**I know practically nothing about some people in this group, I think they must be sad or withdrawn, unable to talk about how they feel.**"

In this example, the perception is of general others in the group. We can follow the example given under Feeling, source specified, by making this other still more generalized, i.e. "People who don't talk must be sad and withdrawn."

Causal Connection

The notion of Causal Connection applies both to feelings and perceptions. It is, however, best illustrated in the Perception context.

Example 1. "**John, you are so aggressive and domineering . . . I think it's because you are really very insecure.**"

In this example, the speaker expresses his perception of the behavior John has exhibited in the group but then goes further to give an additional perception of cause.

Example 2. "**John, you are so aggressive and domineering . . . maybe it's because you feel insecure here or possibly because you've had more group experience.**"

In this example, the speaker suggests possibilities but doesn't own the causal perception or indicate that it is causal by his interpretation.

Example 3. "**John, you are so aggressive . . . maybe there is some reason for that in here.**"

The speaker suggests that there may be some cause but does not suggest one or suggest that he might have one in mind.

Behavior Identified

This is another factor in the openness paradigm which needs further clarification. When behavior is specified in commenting on feelings, when the source is identified, there is less ambiguity and greater clarification as to the source of the feeling and the effect of the feeling in the interactive situation.

Example 1. "Mary, I feel very inferior to you, you seem so capable and self-assured, like when you told us you were an honors student or when you discuss the things you have read in the text."

The behaviors which prompted the feelings in the speaker serve to let Mary know some of the things she does to create the response in the speaker. At the same time, when the behavior is specified, the nature of the feeling is made clearer. The speaker in this example is concerned with intellectual inferiority as a focus, although he may be able to identify others.

Example 2. "Mary, I feel very inferior to you, you seem so capable and self-assured."

In this example Mary can hear that the speaker feels inferior but is unable to understand what aspects of her way of being create that feeling. The speaker, on the other hand, is less open in that he could deny the feedback more easily by saying, ". . . but I guess that is just because I feel inferior today," or something similar. When the behavior is specified, the feeling is anchored to a point in time and a specific act and is less deniable to the speaker.

Openness, as defined, has to do with the degree to which expressions are owned, specific, and unambiguous. Removing statements from the "here and now" makes them more ambiguous. The extent to which expressions are generalized rather than specified relates to the extent to which the speaker expresses ownership of the feeling or perception and the extent to which he is willing to identify those feelings or perceptions with a specific source. Such personal communication is basic and essential for our own self-actualization, as well as the growth of others.

PERSONAL COMMUNICATION IN THE DEVELOPMENT OF SELF

The laboratory group and the behaviors of people in it are tied to certain assumptions of each individual concerning the development and appreciation of "Self." To understand the role that personal communication plays in the process, we shall examine briefly some views of self-concepts.

The main concept of Self is actually composed of many interconnected terms such as self-esteem, self-satisfaction, self-acceptance, and self-favorability. These concepts, which will be discussed later in greater depth, are related to the way in which a person sees himself in terms of those around him.

In a study of "Developmental Changes in the Self Concept" by Long and Associates, seven different components of self were examined. Briefly, these were:

1. Self-esteem—as shown by an individual's self-rating in comparison to others.
2. Dependency—measured by a person's perception of himself as a group member as compared to his perception of himself as an individual.
3. Power of self—as seen in relation to certain authority figures.
4. Centrality—individual's focusing attention upon himself in comparison to his focus of attention on others (i.e. "self-centered").
5. Complexity—differentiation of the self concept, having several motivations for behavior.
6. Individuation—the degree to which an individual differentiates himself from his peers (the counterpoint to dependency).
7. Personal and group identification—measures social distance and inclusiveness.[5]

The interplay between social interactions and self begins when life begins. The child develops a self-concept through his interaction with his family initially and eventually with his peers and teachers. In a theoretical discussion on childhood role taking, Maccoby hypothesized that the greater the frequency of interaction with another person, the greater the possibility that the individual (child) will learn what he has to do to promote harmony in the interaction.[6] This knowledge becomes incorporated in the self-concept.

This role-taking process involves the person's forming a conception of the part he is to play, i.e. his inner definition of what someone in that social position is supposed to think and do. "Role" is the actions of an individual seen in terms of their relevance for the social structure and includes the attitudes, values, and behavior ascribed by the society to any and all persons occupying that particular status. Thus, through role taking, a person incorporates specific values and behavior patterns.

A person's conception of a role, however, may not necessarily coincide with the conception another person has of that role. His individual role performance is his own adjustment depending on the self-concept that he has already formed. It may involve a high or a low degree of self-commitment or personal involvement. Normally, it will not deviate very far from the socially accepted role definition. Thus, a role is a means of manifesting one's self-image and enables a person to interact with others with an anticipation of response.

The way in which a person perceives himself is extremely important in determining his behavior. In addition to his role perception, his perception of (a) his characteristics and abilities, (b) himself in relation to others, (c) himself in relation to the environment, (d) values given to experiences and objects, and (e) negative and positive goals, are all influential in his social interactions.

There is a difference between the concept of a person's *actual* self (i.e. his actual relationships, his actual abilities, etc.) and his *perceived* self. The normal and well-adjusted person will be able to closely coordinate his perception and reality.

In deciding who one is, the importance of personal communication becomes obvious. A person cannot be called good or bad, smart or ignorant, important or insignificant, or given any other qualitative description except in relation to others. This individual's self-rating, referred to as "self-esteem," is a necessity in establishing a self-identity. He must decide where he stands compared to others. The higher he rates himself, the more interaction he will engage in. People with low self-esteem tend to be introverted. They feel they do not have high social approval or recognition and therefore withdraw from social relationships.

Another response of people with low self-esteem is a hesitance in speech labeled "speech anxiety." It is an "unreasonable fear of attempting to communicate in a rather ordinary social situation."[7] As a result, these people withdraw from situations involving social communications. For example, when a person is asked to speak in front of a group of people who are perceived as strangers and who he feels will not accept him as a social equal, he becomes anxious. This anxiety may manifest itself in stuttering, hesitancy, fast talking, quiet tone, or withdrawal.

When withdrawal from interaction involves those with whom one is socially expected to interact, the term "social alienation" is applied. The reason for his breakdown in personal communication may be caused by low self-esteem or extremely high self-esteem (conceit). The main feeling behind either of these explanations is that the people one chooses to avoid interaction with are not capable of providing a satisfying relationship.

One cause of social alienation is "communication denial."[8] When a person's attempt to initiate communication is ignored or not recognized by those he is attempting to communicate with, this is known as "communication denial" and represents a threat to a person's feeling of identity. He has, theoretically, four ways to respond. (1) He can repeat his initial communication attempt; (2) he can demand recognition by speaking louder, more fiercely, making gestures, etc.; (3) he may ask why he is being ignored or refused an answer; (4) he can accept the denial.

If he chooses to repeat his communication and is successful, the effect of the denial will be insignificant. If he becomes aggressive in his communication, this aggression will reach a peak and then turn toward powerlessness. This response is a frustration response and the person who is unsuccessful in overtly trying to attain a response to his communication will most often go to the last alternative and accept the situation and withdraw. Few people have the determination and strength of self-acceptance to actually ask why they are being denied a response. The fear of being in low esteem makes this alternative a rare selection.

The need for social approval is a basic human need. It is contingent to the need for self-esteem in that if a person perceives negative social reactions to him, he finds it comes into conflict with his need for high self-esteem. If this need for self-esteem is greater than the need for social approval, he will tend to raise his self-esteem and have a negative attitude toward society. Because of this negative attitude, he may either act aggressively toward others or choose not to interact with them at all.

A constant need for self-improvement is directly related to the need for self-esteem. People who have a need for high self-esteem are very conscious of their need for self-improvement. They are very aware of reactions of others toward them and of the behavior of others in general. They try to emulate those behaviors which appeal to them most in terms of ego-satisfaction and social acceptance. They strive to follow those behavior patterns which receive the highest social esteem and therefore increase their self-esteem.

Just as there is a difference between perceived role and actual role, there is also a difference between a person's perceived self-esteem and his actual esteem. A person may actually be in a highly accepted social position and therefore be accurate in having a high self-esteem or he may not be in that social position and still have a high self-esteem, consciously or unconsciously, because he has convinced himself. Believing oneself to be in a higher social position than one is actually in is usually a defense mechanism to avoid the pain of reality. A person's awareness of reality and his acceptance of it is therefore very important in understanding his self-concept.

Once a person establishes a level of self-esteem, he will expect certain reactions from others which coincide with that level. If he perceives others as showing greater esteem for him than he does himself, he will either tend to disbelieve these opposing reactions or he will re-evaluate himself. Re-evaluation in this instance would be the most satisfying since it would mean raising one's self-esteem. If a person with a high self-esteem is constantly met with low esteem by others, he has the same two alternatives. In this case, however, it would be more satisfying to withdraw from interaction with those people or to disbelieve them than it would to re-evaluate.

Disbelief of others' reactions can pose a threat to one's self-identity just as communication denial can. It is a matter of how long one can believe that he is right and everyone else is wrong. The need for social approval will drive such a person into an environment where he does get high self-esteem. Thus, for example, a compulsive gambler might find he has high acceptance among his gambler friends but low acceptance among his family and neighbors. Instead of believing his family and re-evaluating himself, he may choose to withdraw from interaction with his family and only interact with other gamblers.

Analysis of this concept of self-esteem uncovers two components —self-confidence and self-security. In order to perceive oneself in relation to others, he must rate himself in terms of *constructiveness* and *elimination of danger.* Constructive activities contribute to greater all-around efficiency. When a person feels he can deal with his surroundings efficiently, he is *self-confident. Self-security* depends on the way one feels he can predict and eliminate danger. This danger is both physical and psychological.

A person with low self-esteem may feel he is unable to function efficiently in comparison to those with whom he interacts. Or, he may feel that his safety is threatened by those around him and he is helpless. Thus the underweight child feels low self-esteem when with others his own age who are capable of beating him up. His security is threatened. In addition, the fact that his friends can lift heavy rocks and he cannot will hurt his self-confidence.

People with low esteem usually are characterized by being either aggressive or withdrawing. This depends on which of the two components of self-esteem are being the most thwarted. If one is frustrated from acting constructively, he becomes aggressive, filled with rage. If he is blocked from feeling secure, he becomes fearful and withdrawing.

Self-esteem expressed in social interaction is often termed *self-assurance*. A person with a lot of self-assurance in his actions is free in his execution of constructive deeds and is relaxed in his relations with others. His emotions of rage and fear are only turned on when appropriate since his normal behavior patterns would not require them.

A person who has assurance will not be hesitant about interpreting the communications of others. He will either trust them or distrust them. Trust is dependent upon one's perception of another's ability to perform a specific function and on how that performance affects the trusting person's self-concept. For example, a boy may know that his teacher is capable of providing information but if he feels that, in the interaction between himself and the teacher, his own capabilities are doubted or are stifled, he will tend to distrust that teacher. If he is constantly fearful of punishment from that teacher, he will have another reason for distrust.

There are some normal situations in which one does not trust the communication he hears because of conflicting beliefs in the intentions of the communicator. Ordinarily, the message would be received favorably, in terms of confidence and security, but in these situations, the receptor senses something conflicting between what is said and what is meant. For example, a boy asks his mother if he may go to the movies. His mother replies, "Yes," but the child perceives this answer as being somewhat hesitant or uncertain. There is a degree of distrust involved.

In an open communication, this child would be able to ask his mother if something were wrong and thereby clarify the answer. If the communication is closed, for any of several reasons, a different situation occurs. The child does not know how to react. If he is unable to get a clarification, the choices previously mentioned as belonging to communication denial situations will also be suitable here. The child feels a two-way pull—in one direction, he wants to go to the movies and has received verbal approval, in the other direction, he has perceived a nonverbal communication which warns him of trouble if he does go. This situation is known as a *double-bind*. It is similar to a situation involving communication denial except that there is an element of trust involved. The person is expected to trust the communications he receives and cannot withdraw from the situation. His difficulty is in interpreting the communication. Where double-binding is of long duration, the person in the midst of this paradox may suffer from insecurity. He has expected a certain response but has not gotten it on a nonverbal level although verbally he has. His trust in the communicator is shaken. He may try to achieve a clarification, as in the communication denial situation, but once he feels distrust, he may not be satisfied by further communications.

Thus, in interpersonal relations *trust* plays a major role. The trusting person expects certain responses in order to achieve some objective. He feels that if his trust is violated, he will suffer a loss. This loss may be in terms of self-image. A person relies upon another to bolster his self-concept and if he does not get this bolstering, he feels distrustful.

Thus, the variables which affect the trust a person will put into a certain situation are (1) self-concept, (2) ability to communicate, and (3) degree of social alienation. A person will not trust those people or situations that threaten to contradict his self-concept. He will also not trust situations or people if he feels there is a lack of clear communications. Third, whereas a person might have alienated himself originally because of distrust, this alienation serves to foster additional feelings of distrust.

In order to keep within the confines of reality, a person cannot only have relationships of distrust. He will tend to seek out those persons whom he can trust and who, significantly, have trust in him. When a person has the trust of his peers, his self-esteem is elevated. His identity is validated through trust also; he feels that others are aware of his existence. Thus, trusting and being trusted are both important to maintaining a self-image.

In seeking trust and social approval, individuals find themselves drawn into groups. These groups have one or more common goals, i.e. the objectives of the group are the objectives of the individual. In order to reach these objectives, the members of the group must conform to certain standards of behavior. A person with a weak self-image (i.e. dependency) will strictly adhere to the group norms because it will give him strength (i.e. reinforce the motives for his behavior). People with a good deal of self-assurance will tend to accept only those group standards which already coincide with their own standards. Too much group conformity tends to diminish the importance of Self. The "over-conformist" loses his self-identity except in terms of the group; his confidence depends upon the acceptance of his conformity.

Many people are unaware of the interplay between their self-concepts and their interpersonal relationships. Their inability to accept reality or to engage in satisfactory relationships may be due to deficient self-concepts. Within a laboratory training group these people have the opportunity to re-evaluate and change their self-images.

One aim of the laboratory group is to make the members extremely aware of the feelings and emotions in themselves and others and thus establish realistic self-concepts. Basically, the group is composed of a small number of people (10–12) and a facilitator who subtly guides the group. In place of ordinary social conversation and small talk, participants of the group begin reacting to one another in deep and significant ways. Complete openness is aimed for and the facilitator only serves to guide, not to lead. After a preliminary period of caution, participants usually feel free to level with one another and voice their true opinions. This freedom to express what one really thinks and feels is based on trust in the group. There is no fear of punishment for honesty.

There are several important foci of this training: (1) the emphasis is on the present situation, not the past life of any of the members or even their present life outside the group; (2) the focus is more upon personal growth and increased human potential than upon corrective treatment; (3) interactions among all group members equally are more important than leader-member relationships; (4) more importantance is given to conscious feelings and motivations than those at an unconscious level; (5) the aim of the group is oriented more toward new *behavior* patterns rather than new motivations; (6) the immediate intent of the facilitator is to improve effectiveness of behavior or change the behavior of the people in the group rather than change personality structure; and (7) the members see themselves as normal people seeking to function more effectively at the interpersonal level rather than as abnormal people seeking treatment.

SUMMARY

In conclusion, a person cannot establish a self-concept without engaging in interpersonal relationships. He must form a perception of himself in relation to others, how others see him and how he sees them. He adapts his behavior patterns to his perceptions and withdraws from situations which would conflict with his self-concept.

In the search for social approval, a person enters many different group relationships. These relationships should be beneficial or he will leave the group and seek another. Members of a group should be aware of each other's needs and opinions as well as their own. They should be able to become interdependent upon each other to support their self-concepts, but their self-concepts should be strong enough to exist without this support. Dependency can weaken a self-image; the person no longer exists as one being alone—he has no identity without the person he has become dependent upon. An individual must accept himself as a human being. He must appraise himself and realize both his desirable and undesirable traits. Only in this way can he engage in interpersonal relationships that will be mutually beneficial.

3

тне procεss of dεvεlopinq a rεlationship

The primary purpose of encounter groups or laboratory training in human relations, as we see it, is to help the participants to improve their ability to develop satisfying relationships with other people. For this improvement in ability to take place, it is helpful to achieve insight into the process by which such relationships are developed. Personal communication plays a decisive role in this process.

In the present chapter we will attempt to analyze the process by which interpersonal relationships are developed and the way in which personal communication contributes to this process.

THE BASIC PROCESS

We interact with other people because we need to, as we have observed in the previous chapter. Even where we are fearful of doing so, we tend to follow the rule of the interpersonal imperative and do our best in socializing and negotiating with others.[1]

As you meet another person for the first time you carry along with you your own needs for interaction; perceiving these needs of your own is the first step in the process of forming a satisfying relationship. Second, you perceive the potential of the other person for satisfying these needs. Some people tend to slight the next two steps in the process, thus antagonizing persons with whom they interact; for a fully satisfying relationship to develop, steps three and four are critical. The third step is to perceive the interpersonal needs of the other person. Step four is to perceive one's own ability to satisfy the other person's needs. The satisfactory use of this four-step process requires that we be able to perceive our needs and the needs of others accurately, and to assess our and their abilities to satisfy these needs.

Perceiving Our Own Interpersonal Needs

Many of us go along day by day seeking to satisfy our needs without taking a very careful look at them. Once in a while we find ourselves in a situation such as the following:

Jim: All the instructor told us to do was to take these soda-pop straws and build some kind of little house.

Joe: I know, but shouldn't we try to make it look like a real house if we can?

Jim: That's okay. But what bothers me is that you seem to think we must try to do it your way. Don't you think some of the rest of us have any good ideas?

Joe: What do you mean by that?

Jim: Well, it seems to me that you are trying to direct this project! You have an idea and you want us to help you carry it out regardless of any ideas of our own.

Joe: I really didn't mean to sound like that. I certainly didn't think of myself as demanding that you do something you don't want to do. What do you want to do?

In many cases we become more aware of our own interpersonal needs if the other person or persons tell us about their impressions of how we behave. In the above example, Joe did have a plan which he wanted carried out by the group; what he didn't realize was that to Jim he seemed to be controlling their behavior despite their personal desires.

Many times we may be unaware of our demands on others, our manipulative behaviors, our "arm-around-the-shoulder" method of getting others to do what we want. We become aware of such behaviors only when others call them to our attention.[2] Participation in human relations laboratory training groups has been shown to increase a person's awareness of his own interpersonal needs.[3]

Our interpersonal needs usually take one or more of these three forms: (1) need to be *included* in social interaction with others; (2) need to reach agreements with others on who is going to *control* whom under what conditions; and (3) need to give and receive *affection* (or at least a need to reduce interpersonal hostility).[4] For each of us, one or more of these needs will be important. Many of us tend to meet and interact with others while only dimly aware of what we want from them. Sometimes we wonder why people aren't friendlier or more considerate, little realizing that in our behavior we are showing them interpersonal needs that they are unable or unwilling to meet. Determining the extent of each of the needs we are carrying around (for example, a need to be shown affection) is the first step toward establishing a satisfactory relationship with another person.

Perceiving the Potential of Others to Meet Our Needs

In many cases we tend to presume that other people can readily meet our interpersonal needs. Actually two problems are involved: (1) we need to make a careful estimate of another person's *capability* of meeting our needs, and (2) we must consider their *willingness* to use this capability.

It should be quite obvious that not just anyone is capable of satisfying someone else's needs. For example, you may have a need for affection; this need can be met to your satisfaction only by people who have certain characteristics that are important to you. Your need for love can hardly be satisfied by just any man or woman you happen to meet. Many of our acquaintances are highly attracted to and seek affection from persons who show them little affection. At the same time, affection easily available from "others" is often spurned or ignored. Romantic novels often display these situations and we easily identify with such behavior. Most notable, perhaps, are the unsatisfied needs for affection depicted in the novel *Gone with the Wind*.

An accurate estimate of another person's capacity for meeting our interpersonal needs is handicapped if we are not fully aware of what our needs are. Awareness is enhanced by interaction experience involving feedback on how we are seen by others.[5] The estimate can be accurate only if the opportunity to interact with the other person is available. In simple language, "we have to get to know him." Experiencing interaction with another person in the exploratory phase of a relationship is somewhat like "trying it on for size." For example, we may be very much attracted to a person; we may think we like him very much; our early interactions may show some signs of his capacity to satisfy our need for affection. At the same time, however, we may be quite surprised or even shocked by our negative reactions to his efforts to control our behavior. He may be entirely unable to meet our need for independence or at least our need to *share* control over each other.[6] At this point we should observe that the process of establishing a relationship requires that we note carefully not only how we behave together but also how we feel about each other.[7]

In some cases other people may be incapable of satisfying one or more of our interpersonal needs; in other cases they may be quite capable, but unwilling. Their willingness will be influenced by their motivations based upon their own interpersonal needs. The degree to which their needs are satisfied will be compared by them to the cost or investment of their time and energy required to get us to meet their needs. The principle exposed here is one of social exchange or cost/reward ratio, which will be discussed in greater detail after we look at the two other factors in the process of establishing a relationship.

Perceiving Interpersonal Needs of Others

A relationship cannot be established if we cannot meet some of the interpersonal needs of the other person. We may dimly perceive these needs by observing how he behaves. In so doing we run the risk of having our inferences distorted by our own perceptual filters. We see one another through a lens developed by our own unique experiences; this lens or filter is also somewhat distorted by our own needs and desires.[8]

Our observations need to be enhanced by statements from the other person regarding his perception of his needs. His statements may not be entirely accurate, of course, if he is not well aware of these needs; in addition, he may not be willing to give us completely truthful statements even if he is aware of his needs.[9] He may fear the consequences of exposing his inner needs; he may fear us in particular or people in general.[10]

The interaction procedures usually used in encounter groups or training groups in human relations are specially designed to overcome these problems.[11] In such laboratory groups exposure of interpersonal needs and sharing perceptions of them is ordinarily a major focus of the work of the group.[12]

We have noted that we can detect some clues regarding the inter-personal needs of others by observing their behavior while being aware of the possible distortion of our own perceptual lens. We have further noted that we can ask them to tell us of their needs, being aware as we listen that they may not know them well and, in addition, may be unwilling to describe them truthfully. In the long run, however, we can get our best estimate by noting the way they respond to our efforts to meet these needs. For example, we may become convinced that they need affection or sympathy; however, if when offered it is rejected, we must conclude that they don't want it—at least, not from us at this time.[13]

Estimating Our Potential for Satisfying the Interpersonal Needs of Others

How can we tell when we are meeting others' needs? As suggested above, we can observe their behavior and we can ask them to tell us —in both cases exercising due consideration for distortion or incomplete data. Also, as suggested above, we can note their responses to our efforts to meet their needs.

An interpersonal relationship is a personal matter. For example, it may be impossible for anyone else but your father, mother, husband, or wife to meet one or another of your needs. Some other need may not possibly be met by any of them—only by a good friend of your age and sex.

The dynamics of a personal relationship are such that a show of affection by one person frequently does not make us feel the same emotion as does a demonstration of affection from someone else.[14] Thus, *the way we feel* when some other person attempts to meet our interpersonal needs is extremely important. Is it possible to communicate these feelings to the other person in the relationship?

Obviously such communication is impossible if the other person is not interested or will not (or cannot) "tune in" or listen. But how should we listen? What should we be sure to hear or understand? Special procedures that help us to be more aware of our own feelings as well as the feelings of others have been developed by persons experienced in leading laboratory groups in human relations training.[15] These procedures will be discussed in some detail in the next major section of this chapter. At this point, however, let's take a careful look at the four elements of the process of developing a relationship, noting how they relate to or interact one with another.

Applying the Principle of Social Exchange

As we start to form a relationship with another person we employ all four of the steps discussed above almost simultaneously. We encounter the other person with at least some awareness of our own needs, although our attention will likely be focused on cues for estimating his needs. We form a quick estimate of his potential for meeting our needs and constantly revise this estimate as we get to know more about him. At the same time we make and revise our estimate of our potential for satisfying his needs.

In estimating his and our potential for satisfying each other's interpersonal needs, we are concerned with (1) capability and (2) willingness. For example, you may have the capability to meet my need for receiving affection, but be unwilling to give me that much affection. Willingness to meet the interpersonal needs of another person is based upon a comparison of (1) cost to us in time and energy, with (2) degree to which our own needs will be satisfied. Two well-known psychologists, John Thibaut and Harold Kelley have identified this principle as the consideration of the cost/reward ratio. They summarize its use in this fashion:

If both persons are able to produce their maximum rewards for the other at the minimum cost to themselves, the relationship will not only provide each with excellent reward-cost positions but will have the additional advantage that both persons will be able to achieve their best reward-cost positions at the same time.[16]

Working independently but at about the same time, another social-psychologist, George Homans, elaborated much the same analysis of the development of human relationships; he called it a "theory of social exchange."[17] Although Homans' theory differs in some detail from that of Thibaut and Kelley, they agree remarkably in essential principles.[18]

The continuation of a relationship, once initiated, will depend upon the cost/reward ratio for either participant. If, for either one, the perceived costs significantly exceed the perceived rewards, the relationship is not likely to endure.[19] As a relationship grows and develops we tend to explore the possible values. We experience samples of what can happen, and we note trends, deriving what can be called an estimate of the relationship potential.[20]

Human beings, like all animal species, have a way of communicating their needs and the degree to which these needs are being met.[21] For us humans this communication system consists of all our behavior, verbal and nonverbal, vocal and nonvocal.[22] It includes words, phrases, and sentences; in addition, it involves vocal intonations, gleeful noises, moans, gestures, posture, eye glances, glares, and laughter.[23] On a street corner in Detroit or Boise or Burma or Nigeria, a mother may sit on the cold curb trying to cuddle and warm her child. The silent message of a mother with her child is recognized and respected all over the world. Another world-respected principle of human interaction is that if a person *gives* something he will almost always expect something in return—at least some recognition and consideration.[24]

In a human relationship, costs to an individual consist of investment of time and energy; embarrassment, anxiety, love, and anger are all examples of psychological costs.[25] Rewards consist of being included in the interactions of others, reaching agreements upon control of and by others, and giving and/or receiving affection.[26] The value of one or another of these rewards will vary considerably from one person to another; each individual's use of these factors to determine his own cost/reward ratio in a relationship will be almost unique to that person.[27]

In a human relationship the persons involved may change somewhat over time in order to accommodate the interpersonal needs of each other. Behaviors that elicit desired rewards tend to be repeated; costly behaviors are avoided and tend to diminish.[28] In this fashion the relationship tends to stabilize and be more satisfying; if such is not the case, the relationship is often diminished or discontinued.

At any given time in one of our relationships with another person, his cost/reward ratio will be exceedingly important to us if we want that relationship to continue. However, we can know this condition of the other person only to the extent that he communicates it to us. We can listen very carefully to their words; we can find ways of encouraging them to disclose verbally more of their perceptions of us along with other feelings about these perceptions. We can more easily note their facial expressions, gestures, postures, signs of body tension, and other nonverbal ways of communicating their feelings.[29] To a very large extent learning to be more aware of these elements of interpersonal communication is the essence of training in human relations.[30]

Information regarding how a person perceives us and how he feels about these perceptions is very personal in nature. People do not tend to communicate these data to just any other person.[31] The exchange of such information can very properly be called personal communication. It is highly essential to the process of forming a satisfactory, continuing relationship with another person; in fact, as we see it, it is the essence of this process. The next section of this chapter focuses on this kind of communication.

THE ROLE OF PERSONAL COMMUNICATION

The essential requirements for establishing a satisfactory, lasting relationship, as we have seen, are (1) to be aware of our own interpersonal needs, (2) to perceive accurately that the other person is able and willing to meet these needs, (3) to perceive accurately the interpersonal needs of the other person, and (4) to be able and willing to meet these needs. In addition, for either us or them, the costs involved must not appear to be greater than the rewards derived.

As you try to perceive the needs of another person and his ability or willingness to satisfy your needs, communication of these factors is of critical importance. You need to compare your perceptions with those of the other person; also, you need to compare your feelings about those perceptions with his feelings. These items of information will be communicated to some extent by nonvocal or nonverbal means whether we wish them to be disclosed or not. They can be communicated much more clearly if (1) we are willing to disclose such information one to another, and (2) if we are honest in these disclosures. Personal communication of this kind is somewhat rare and ordinarily viewed as risky. Even so, such disclosing behavior can be increased by training which provides better ways of judging the degree of risk involved.[32]

Comparing Our Perceptions with Those of Others

Most of us carry around with us an image of ourselves. Included in this self-image is a view of our interpersonal needs.[33] To a very great extent other people will be willing to form a relationship with us depending upon their perception of our needs. If *our* image of our needs is significantly different from *their* perception of these needs, we will tend to be disappointed in seeking to establish satisfactory relations with others; in addition, we will be left wondering why we are so unsuccessful.[34] If you interact in certain ways with your mother, does this make her feel happy? Are you sure? Do you know what you do that makes your wife or husband feel sad? Angry? Happy? If you are not married, can you answer similar questions regarding your interactions and the feelings of a close friend? The man or woman you are dating? planning to marry?

The first objective of personal communication in establishing a relationship will be to disclose to another person your view of your interpersonal needs and to ask for his perceptions of these needs.[35] These items of information may be given in about this way:

Don: I don't see myself as needing a lot of affection but I do know that I don't like to have other people tell me what to do.

Helen: Well, I agree with you that you don't like to be controlled, but I see you as needing quite a bit of personal warmth and attention.

Don: You do? Needing quite a bit of affectionate attention?

Helen: Yes. When you present your ideas you really don't seem to mind if I disagree with them provided I don't give you the impression I dislike you. In fact, it seems necessary to be sure I maintain some show of regard or warmth as I disagree with your viewpoint. I saw this causing us some difficulty yesterday. Right now, I sense that you are a little bothered that I am disagreeing with your view of yourself, and I want you to know that I still like you as much as ever.

Don: I'm glad you said that. For more than one reason. I can better understand your responses to me in light of your perceptions of me. Also, you're right—I was a little bothered that maybe you didn't like what you saw in me as a need for affection. My being bothered about this tends to prove your point, doesn't it?

Comparing Feelings about Interpersonal Perceptions

The second objective of personal communication in establishing a desirable relationship is to compare *feelings* about our interpersonal perceptions. It is not enough simply to compare perceptions; we must be aware of how we feel about them and how the other person feels about them. In the example given above, it was very important for Don to know *how Helen felt* about her perception of his need for affection. Did she dislike it? Resent it? Feel that it might be too costly to her in terms of time and energy?

The following example may help to provide further insight regarding the importance of comparing our own feelings with those of the other person:

Sherry: I know I like to see things accomplished. I'm the sort of person who dislikes indecision and needless delay. I'm willing to work hard but I want to see some action. I don't mind making suggestions so long as it leads to something useful.

Mike: I know you are a very dynamic person who is willing to make suggestions and work hard to achieve results. I also see you as being quite aggressive in the leadership role; you don't exactly push people around but you tend to get them moving.

Sherry: Do you dislike these qualities in me? Does this behavior irritate you or make you feel angry toward me?

Mike: Only rarely. Most of the time I like to have you get me and others into action. Someone has to show some interest and desire or we'd never get anything done. But once in awhile your pushiness does bother me and then I resent your demanding behavior.

Sherry: I really did wonder about that. At times I thought you felt negative toward me, but I wasn't sure because at other times you seemed to respond favorably to my behavior. Would you give me some firm indication the next time I overdo it and you feel dissatisfied with my action?

Mike: Well, if you really want me to, I will.

Sherry: I really want to know. It can help us get along better, don't you think?

Mike: Yes, if you really do pay attention and ease up a bit when I feel you are going too far.

Sherry: I'd like to try that and see how it works out.

It should be obvious that, in order for us to compare our self-perceptions with others' perceptions of us, we must first interact with one another. Also, of course, such interaction is necessary if we are going to *compare our feelings regarding our behavior with feelings generated in others.*

It is very important to note that the optimum value of sharing our perceptions and feelings can only be achieved if we interact in numerous different kinds of situations and settings. These situations can include work and play as well as conditions wherein we are relaxed; also, interaction that generates tension should be included. The wider the range and scope of such activities, the more valuable can such shared information be toward establishing a viable relationship.[36] This will be particularly true to the extent that the interactions in which two people engage are relevant to the kind of relationship they wish to establish; for a dating or courting relationship, working together may not be very important. However, before marriage is seriously considered, interacting in a work relationship is very important unless the marriage is expected to consist only of fun and games.[37]

Attempting Change with Feedback

As the members of a relationship continue to communicate perceptions of each other and their feelings about these perceptions, they
may find that their attitudes toward themselves are changing. Parts
of their self-images may seem less attractive; they may desire to seek
to change their own behavior.[38]

An attempt to change one's interpersonal behavior should never
be tried unless one is personally convinced of the merit of the
change. It should not be tried if it is not desired by the person
involved, especially if requested by the other person and not fully
accepted by the one attempting to change.[39] In no case should such
attempts to change be primarily motivated by manipulation or coercion on the part of the other person; such efforts are usually doomed
to failure and serious damage to the relationship can occur. Berne's
descriptions of "games" people play provides considerable support
for this conclusion.[40] The primary value one of us can be to another
who is attempting to change his interpersonal behavior is to give him
feedback regarding his efforts. In this way we can help him to evaluate his relative success or failure in his attempts to change.[41]

We should note at this point that feedback regarding attempted
changes will, once again, consist essentially of our perceptions of that
person's behavior and our feelings regarding it. We will need to
communicate to him these perceptions and feelings. The essence of
this procedure will be personal communication, and the other person's satisfaction with changes attempted will be heavily influenced
by our ability to engage in such communication.[42]

The kind of personal communication envisioned in this section is
not easy and tends to go against years of experience and training in
our childhood where we learned to keep others from knowing how
we saw them and felt about them.[43] Only by deliberate, planned
effort are we ordinarily able to overcome this training and our fear
of revealing ourselves to others. As we see it, such deliberate effort
is the essence of human relations training in encounter or laboratory
groups.[44] In the next section of this chapter we take a careful look
at the training procedure involved.

THE ESSENCE OF THE ENCOUNTER GROUP EXPERIENCE

The essential element of human relations training in encounter or
laboratory groups consists of personal communication regarding how

we are seen and how others feel about their perception of us. This is best accomplished when certain communication behaviors are achieved: perceptions and feelings are honestly presented; these perceptions and feelings relate to experiences common to the interacting participants; and one's own perceptions and feelings are openly admitted.[45] These items of information are presented, of course, on the basis of experienced interaction with one another.

Experiencing Interaction

The history of the movement to improve human relations supports the principle that the best progress can be made when people interact in encounter groups or laboratory training groups; it is not easy to improve one's human relations skill just by reading a book.[46] In order for useful perceptions and feelings to be shared, people must interact, giving to one another appropriate bases for interpersonal perceptions and feelings.[47] If you and I do not interact with one another, if you can't tell how I ordinarily behave and if I can't determine the kind of responses my behavior generates in you, then we cannot share useful information about our personal perceptions and feelings.

For me to obtain a better understanding of behavior of mine that limits or damages my efforts to establish a satisfying relationship with others, some others must witness my behavior and note their feelings about it. To the extent that my behavior in their presence is similar to my *usual* or *habitual* behavior, I can learn what I ordinarily do that is valuable and/or dysfunctional. To the extent that all relevant conditions of my life-interactions are replicated in the laboratory group, my learning can be generalized to my various life-situations.[48]

Achieving Interpersonal Trust

To improve our ability to relate to others, it is not enough that we simply interact in our usual way; we must know how we are being perceived by others and how they feel about us. We can draw some useful inferences just by noting their responses to us; however, we can learn more if they tell us directly and honestly their perceptions and feelings. In order for this degree of openness and honesty to prevail, a climate of interpersonal trust must be achieved.[49]

In order for people to trust one another they must come to appreciate each other as (1) reliable, (2) intelligent or knowledgeable, and (3) dynamic.[50] They must see each other as dependable, and they will need to answer these questions about one another in the affirmative: Can I reveal my ideas and beliefs without getting hurt? Will I be accepted as I am without having to change myself in ways I don't wish? Can I depend upon them not to take advantage of my confidences, my exposure of myself, for their selfish use or manipulation of me? In a large study of a number of training groups, Jack Gibb ascertained that this question of acceptance without misuse of exposure of one's idea and beliefs was the first and primary concern of group members.[51]

The members of the training group must come to see each other as intelligent, informed, or knowledgeable. When we see another person as well-informed we tend to do so in our own frame of reference, that is, in ways *we* are informed.[52] We ask these questions: Does he or she know the world as I know it? See it as I see it? Does his or her training and experience lead to the acceptance of major goals in life that are similar to mine? Will he or she have the same goals as I in this specific group or situation? The training group members eventually must see one another as having mutually compatible goals in the training experience if the experience is to be of optimum value.[53]

The third factor in establishing interpersonal trust is a question of dynamism. It may not be as important as the questions of reliability and knowledgeability, but it is important. The specific questions raised about another person are of this order: Will he put forth real effort? When we are in trouble, will he be active in the struggle or will he passively sit by and let us be hurt? Will he act in a crisis?[54]

In the long-range study of training groups conducted by Gibb, a climate of mutual trust had to be achieved or at least substantial progress had to be made in that direction before any of the training goals could be accomplished.[55] This was necessary because improvement in human relations capability is so heavily dependent upon interpersonal feedback; without this use of personal communication the efforts of a training group are severely limited.

Providing Interpersonal Feedback: The Openness Paradigm

The literature on encounter groups frequently suggests interpersonal *openness* as requisite training procedure for improving capability in human relations. Frederick Stoller suggests: "One of the most important group operations consists of having feedback, the specification of the effects one group member has upon another."[56]

Schein and Bennis have argued that practically all of our learning "is based on the idea of obtaining information about our performance and then determining how far our progress deviates from some desired goal."[57]

In chapter 2 we presented a schema representing eight factors seen as supportive to the optimum of openness in personal communication. From that perspective we believe that there are five basic procedures that constitute an operational paradigm of openness. Each of them must be understood clearly if they are to be used to optimum advantage in human relations training; for this reason, we shall discuss each in some detail.

1. Describing mutually shared experiences. In encounter groups one often hears the injunction, "Stay in the here and now." The call is to avoid extensive references to events or experiences not shared by the other members of the group. In the early hours of the life of a group this injunction is very useful. However, as the members spend hours or days together, references to shared experiences in their earlier meetings can also be useful. It then becomes apparent that "here and now" actually relates to experiences mutually shared at any time, if they have some "here and now" significance to the members. For example, insight into an earlier conflict between two members may have relevance here and now if a new conflict appears on the interaction horizon. In essence, any interpersonal event or experience clearly understood by the group members to have *immediate relevance* at any given time may be fruitful for their analysis, interpretation, reinterpretation, and understanding. The event's *relevance at this time* is the optimum criterion for what should be discussed in an encounter group; this decision can best be made by the group members.

2. Describing one's perception of another's behavior. This procedure is the basic operation in the interpersonal feedback process so frequently suggested in human relations training literature.[58] The behavior which another person perceives (and attempts to describe) should be clearly identified; the person whose behavior is perceived (and then described) should also be specified. A poor imitation of this procedure is the following: "Some members of the group have told us very little of what they are thinking; they don't seem to be interested in trying to help us learn." Here the behavior perceived is not specified and the persons behaving are unidentified. Such feedback is of only minimal value. A good example of describing one's perception of another's behavior is the following: "Jane, when you replied to John's question, I saw your response as very authoritative; you tried to tell him what kinds of questions we would allow in our group." Identification of *whose* behavior and *what* behavior can provide feedback that is potentially useful to the person receiving it.

3. Describing one's feelings about another's behavior.   As we have suggested previously, a person may perceive you as a leader in the group and, depending upon his previous experiences or motives at the time, he may approve of your behavior or may feel disgusted, angry, or even resentful. If you are to improve your relationship with that person, not only must you ascertain how he sees you, but what feelings these perceptions have produced. To be of optimum use to you, the behavior generating the feeling should be specified, along with the other person's feeling about it. A poor example of feedback concerning one's interpersonal feeling is the following: "Sometimes people in this group seem angry and very defensive. This makes us uncomfortable." A better attempt could specify the behavior generating interpersonal feeling and more accurately describe the feeling: "Sue, your comment to John made me very angry and defensive; I don't feel like asking your opinion or giving mine after you have attacked one of us that way."

4. Owning one's perceptions of or feelings about another's behavior. In many situations it seems easier to give interpersonal feedback if we clothe our perceptions or feelings in anonymity. Thus, we may suggest that some unidentified "others" see things thus or so, or that "the group" feels a certain way. Such vague suggestions may be of some limited value as feedback, but whenever we hear such deviously implied reactions to our own behavior, we nearly always want to know, "Who saw me that way?" or "Who felt that way about me?" To be of optimal value to us feedback needs to be owned by the person having such perceptions and feelings; we can accept it more comfortably when it applies to us if he will "own up to" his own behavior. Only when we know who is involved can we make a satisfactory assessment of the validity of the suggested response. A poor example of ownership of perception and interpersonal feeling is the following: "Clarence, we don't know whether you like us or not; some of us would like to know how you feel." A better example is this: "Julie, I see you as capable and self-assured; I like the way you stepped into our confused situation and identified our source of conflict."

5. *Describing attributed meaning of another's behavior.* We all attribute to others certain motives and intentions according to our perceptions of their actions; as a matter of fact, we tend to do this whenever we interact with others. In this way we assess the "meaning" of their behavior.

Attribution theory regarding interpersonal relations is, at present, in its very early stages of development. Attribution by one person of motives on the part of another, on the basis of interpersonal perceptions, has been explored by Fritz Heider in his system for "naive" analysis of interpersonal action. In describing the way in which we attribute motives or intentions to the actions of others, he placed special emphasis on two concepts: (1) Is that person *capable* of achieving the attributed purpose or intentions, and (2) does he appear to be *trying* to achieve it.[59] In their elaboration of Heider's approach, Jones and Davis have suggested that we must also estimate the perceived person's *knowledge*. For example, if he does not have knowledge enough to *foresee the effects* of his behavior, we could not properly attribute *intention* to produce such effects.[60] Although attribution theory has been used by Harold Kelley to describe conditions that make a person susceptible to persuasion,[61] our interest here is in factors that help us attribute meaning to a person's perceived responses.

The accuracy with which we attribute motives and intentions to others is a problem greatly in need of further research. However, the fact that we try to guess the reasons underlying the behavior of others is verifiable by any thoughtful observer.

As you note another person's behavior when the two of you are together, it is very helpful toward achievement of a satisfactory relationship if you can ascertain the meaning of his behavior. *It is also very helpful if you can determine what meaning he is attributing to your behavior.* For example, in a friendly way, a man asks a young woman to have lunch with him. He may not focus his attention on it completely, but he will likely note whether she responds to his invitation as if it is a simple, friendly act, or behaves as if he has asked for a "date." What intentions or motives does she seem to be ascribing to his invitation? Would she be upset if he attempted to join casual acquaintances as he chose a table?

A relationship can be facilitated if one person can openly ask the other person regarding the motives or intentions behind certain behaviors. In addition, if the other person seems confused and perhaps embarrassed to ask how we are interpreting his behavior, it is often quite helpful to the relationship if we will simply state our guesses about the meaning of his actions. For example, suppose this situation arose:

John: Molly, I hope you are not bothered about my missing the meeting last night.
Molly: No, it's okay. But we did miss you.

This conversation *could* stop here and John could make *guesses* about how Molly had interpreted his comment. For example, did she think he was apologizing for his absence? Did she think he meant to tell her not to worry about his commitment to the group? Or that reasons for his absence were not for her to worry about, that is, none of her business? Both John's and Molly's sense of their relationship can be clarified if this additional exchange were to occur:

John: Well, I brought it up because I wanted you to know I meant to be there; I'm not angry any more about our little disagreement last time. I wanted to be sure you didn't think I didn't come because of that.
Molly: I wondered about that. I'm glad to know that wasn't it. I want to work together with you on this committee. I think that your experience and my training can both be of real value.

In many cases it can be helpful to a relationship if you indicate your guesses about the motives or intentions behind another person's behavior, even if they don't ask; they may be embarrassed to request such personal information. The following interchange may illustrate this procedure:

Mike: I saw you glaring when I told them I wanted to quit the team. *I suppose you feel I am letting them down and resent my lack of loyalty.*
Bob: I was hoping we could talk about that. No, I'm not upset by your leaving. What bothered me was that they acted as if you didn't have a right to join a better team. I've also been thinking of quitting and I don't think they have a right to try to stop us.
Mike: Well, that certainly makes me feel better. At least you understand what I'm doing. If you decide to quit let's go together and talk to that new Southtown team being organized.

In such a situation we have to recognize, of course, that the other person might not always be telling the truth. Perhaps, in some cases, our first guess (inference or attribution) regarding the meaning of their behavior might actually be correct, even if denied. Even so, to tell the other person *what that guess is,* and to hear them tell us what they *want* us to believe can provide a more useful foundation on which to build a relationship than to try to build it upon unchecked guesses regarding the meaning of various behaviors. The building of a relationship ultimately requires that, in one way or another, by verbal or nonverbal messages, the *meanings* of our interpersonal behaviors must be established. For example, suppose, as Bob shows up late for his date with Jane, this occurs:

Jane: Well, it's about time!

Bob: I know you're upset with me. I'm sorry I'm late. I know you're irritated at missing the others. We'll try to catch them at the clubhouse.

Jane would feel differently about their relationship if, instead of the sequence above, the following had been Bob's response:

Jane: Well, it's about time!

Bob: So you're angry. There you go again. I'll bet it's caused by your female envy of my being a man. You women always think you can be late, but you raise a fuss every time a man isn't right on time!

In this case, it is doubtful if they will catch up with Ted and Alice at the clubhouse.

At this point it should be noted that all five of the procedures we have listed in the openness paradigm involve personal communication from one member of a group to another. In a laboratory training group each of these procedures can be practiced as an interpersonal relation's skill, later to be used from time to time in establishing more satisfactory human relations.

The University of Kansas has established a program of instruction in communication in human relations starting at the undergraduate level and leading to a Doctor of Philosophy degree. Each year for over ten years hundreds of students have enrolled in the primary orientation course which is a laboratory group experience. Numerous experimental studies have evaluated the success of this course in meeting its objectives. For the most part these studies have shown positive results.[62] Careful observation of a number of these training groups has suggested the importance of the five procedures we have identified as the openness paradigm. In addition, an experimental study by MacDoniels has demonstrated that members of training groups can be trained to improve significantly in these behaviors during the course of three or four brief meetings together.[63]

Determining Group Perceptions and Feelings

We are quite aware that an *individual's* perceptions or feelings concerning the behavior of another person may be significantly limited or distorted by his own interpersonal needs or previous experiences. Thus, as you obtain feedback concerning your interpersonal behavior, you must consider it *only tentatively valid.* You must, in addition, be concerned regarding the truthfulness of the feedback given; even if another person perceives you accurately, he may be unwilling to speak in all honesty.

To some extent these handicaps can be overcome by having a *number* of persons observe your behavior and compare their responses.[64] It is, of course, quite possible that after two or three group members have agreed upon their perceptions, few people will want to offer disagreeing statements.[65] Even so, there is some safety in numbers *when the members of the group are aware of the importance to you of each individual person's reaction, and that agreeing dishonestly can be a great disservice to you or another group member.* To the extent that your group understands the significance of such feedback to personal growth in human relations capability, and to the extent that they are committed to helping one another achieve such growth, they can "sit as a jury" in giving their perceptions of and feelings about your actions. In this way an encounter group experience can be of great value to a group member, providing him with more dependable information about how he is perceived and received by others.

Preserving a Person's Option for Change

On occasion we have seen a number of the more vocal members of a group demanding that a selected group member change his ways; we have been reminded of scenes of Simon Legree pursuing Little Eva across the ice. We object to a group's making such demands of its members on four counts.

In the first place, such scenes are highly emotionalized ones for the person under attack and do not strike us as being good learning experiences. After such an event the victim is likely to remember his feelings of fear of the group and be unable to reflect reasonably upon the behavior in question.[66] He may learn to avoid obtaining useful feedback instead of learning to use it for his own growth.

In the second place, we must keep in mind that not all people see us accurately and some are only partly honest in voicing their perceptions. Three very vocal members demanding that we change may not be speaking correctly for the other silent members of the group.

In the third place, for a change in interpersonal behavior to be anything other than temporary, it must be fully desired by the changing person; any private reservations or hesitations on his part can make such a change of short endurance.[67] Sometime later it may be easier to find other people with whom he can be somewhat congenial than it is to change to suit a few members of a training group. Changing one's way of interacting with people is not an easy task at best. It is almost impossible if the individual involved is not sincerely dedicated to its achievement.[68]

As a fourth consideration we suggest that a person's image of his interpersonal behavior is very important to his sense of personal well-being. To be confronted with information that diminishes this self-image immediately calls forth impulses of self-defense.[69] If the behavior in question truly is ineffective or dysfunctional, one's defense of it is usually not very valid, sometimes not even reasonable. In such a case it is quite easy for the group members to tear down these defenses, pointing out how they are irrational, not based upon reality. When this line of defense goes, an individual is usually under severe strain or tension. Severe emotional upset, even emotional breakdown, can result.[70] As we see it, the desirable use of the openness paradigm is to *offer a group member information so long as he wants it and indicates he will give it his consideration*. After he has been given these data he should be allowed to consider it without group pressure. Demands for change should be avoided by the group; pressure from the group leader, either explicit or implicit, for individual change appears to us to be more harmful than useful.[71] Even if such pressures are activated only by *emulation* of the leader and high regard for his evaluation, they appear to do more harm than good.[72]

Supporting Efforts When Change Is Attempted

When feedback has been given, and when the recipient decides that he *wants* to change his behavior, a very useful function can be performed by the group in giving support for changes attempted. Two different aspects of this support can be helpful.

In the first place, any *attempt* to change can be given favorable reinforcement even if the attempt is weak and the immediate change is negligible. Support for a person's effort, even if not very successful, can encourage that effort to continue. In the second place, a person will need to know how he is doing as seen by friendly others.

As he attempts to change, it will be helpful to know if others perceive the change and how they feel about the new behavior. At this point, the five elements of the openness paradigm again become very useful. Progress in changing will of necessity be gauged by the nature of the feedback received. Once again, the role of personal communication in human relations training becomes paramount.

In this chapter we have stressed the importance of *feedback* in establishing satisfactory human relations as well as learning how to improve our ways of relating to others. In stressing the importance of personal communication for these purposes we may have unwittingly left the impression that such communication consists essentially of vocal-verbal interaction. We have not meant to create such an impression.

Personal communication as feedback for establishing relationships or improving our capability to achieve them involves all the nonverbal, nonvocal means as well as the use of spoken words. Neither mode of behavior should be neglected.

In the literature of encounter groups and in the practice of group leaders or trainers, considerable emphasis is placed upon one person physically touching another.[73] Our own experience and observation leads us to believe that touching another person is a very important part of the process of relating to that person, probably for two reasons.

In the first place many people in our present culture are apparently very lonely in the personal psychological sense. They long to be closer to somebody; when they can physically reach out and touch someone, this need for psychological closeness seems, in part, to be met. This, of course, is true only if the individual touched responds favorably and welcomes such psychological closeness. We do not hold that just any group of a dozen people can be brought together and asked to reach out and touch each other with any guarantee of positive results. However, we have seen positive results so many times that we believe, in our society, the interpersonal need is quite prevalent.[74]

In the second place, touching someone and noting his response is a very helpful way of checking on his verbal-vocal messages. Empirical research data tends to confirm this observation. Common experience also lends it considerable support. A mother can usually tell when a temporary clash with her child has been forgotten by the way the child responds to her touch. If someone tells us he loves us but stiffens or turns away when we touch his hand we know we have to reconsider his words.[75] One of the present authors, through years of experience as a horse trainer, has learned that he can best tell "where he is" with an animal by touching its neck or shoulder and noting the degree of friendliness, fear, or resentment in its response; the degree of muscular tension can actually be felt as an index of the horse's attitude.

At least one study has shown that interpersonal relations can be assessed and improved significantly through use of the sense of touch.[76] It is our belief that its primary value is as a means of gaining feedback regarding how we are perceived by others and the way they feel about how they see us.

SUMMARY

In this chapter we have suggested that our individual interpersonal needs motivate us to interact with other persons. In order to meet these needs on a routine basis we seek to establish workable, stable, satisfactory relationships.

We have identified four elements in the basic process of developing an interpersonal relationship: (1) perceiving our own interpersonal needs; (2) estimating the potential of the other person (or persons) to satisfy our needs; (3) perceiving the interpersonal needs of the other person (or persons); and (4) estimating our potential for satisfying their needs. As these perceptions and estimates are made, each person in the relationship constantly applies the principle of social exchange; he mentally calculates the ratio between his personal costs and rewards. Will he receive an equivalent for his investment of time and energy? If he thinks not—if he thinks his costs will exceed his rewards—he will tend to diminish or terminate the relationship.

In establishing a satisfactory human relationship the role of personal communication is paramount. We employ it in three ways: (1) we compare our perceptions of our own interpersonal behavior with feedback from others regarding how they see us; (2) we compare how we feel about our behavior with how others tell us they feel about it; and (3) if we attempt to change, we listen to the feedback from others regarding the way these attempted changes are seen and the feelings they produce.

We have suggested that the essence of the encounter group or laboratory training group experience consists of feedback regarding our interpersonal behavior. First, we interact with others to allow them to experience our interpersonal behavior. Second, valid feedback requires that the group members achieve, so far as possible, a climate of interpersonal trust. Third, the members engage in personal communication. In this procedure we have described a *paradigm of openness in interaction*: (1) group members describe mutually shared interpersonal experiences: mainly these relate to "the here and now"; (2) members describe the perceived behavior of one another; (3) they describe their feelings about these perceived behaviors; (4) they identify perceptions and feelings that are their own—they "own up to" having them; and (5) they describe causes, motives, or intentions *attributed* to others as underlying these perceived behaviors.

The fourth essential element of the encounter group experience is determining group perceptions and feelings regarding any one item of behavior exhibited by a member. There is some safety in numbers as we obtain feedback from others provided they are (1) aware of the importance of each member being honest and (2) committed to giving one another this kind of feedback.

The fifth essential element of encounter group training is that of preserving the individual's personal option to decide to try—or not to try—to change in line with the feedback he has received. Without personal commitment such attempts will likely be ineffective; attempts produced by interpersonal pressure, even if only by emulation of an idealized leader, may be psychologically harmful.

The sixth and final element we regard as essential is that the group members support an individual's efforts to change if and when he decides to do so in response to the feedback he has been given.

The behaviors involved in *establishing* a relationship are strikingly similar to essential elements in encounter group or laboratory group training. To a large extent they consist of personal communication in the form of feedback. These are the primary behaviors we have identified as the openness paradigm. As we see it, *personal growth in human relations capability* rests squarely on effective use of interpersonal feedback.

4

THE RELATIONSHIP PARADIGM

A person tries to satisfy his interpersonal needs by establishing relationships with other people. We have seen in chapter 3 how a person ordinarily goes about this process.

In many cases people attempt to build rewarding relationships with whomever happens to be nearby—members of the immediate family, school classmates, college roommates, the boy or girl next door. Such relationships appear to be based upon convenience; many times they are not stable or very rewarding. In some cases the relationship may have started well and brought early signs of interpersonal reward; then, after a time, it became rigid, sterile, unrewarding. For the most part, in developing our interpersonal relationships, we tend to do the best we can, riding out emotional storms, accommodating others whenever possible or when we feel like it, and hoping for the best.

One of the primary goals of many encounter groups is for the participants to take a careful look at themselves and the ways in which they relate to other people. When this is done, what are they looking for? Our interactions are composed of a hundred or more different behaviors; for example, our eyes meet; we smile; we say,

"How are you?" Sometimes we act as if we really care. We eat together, work together. We pass one another in the hall or on the sidewalk. We arrange a date to go to lunch, or dinner, or a movie. On that date we meet, we smile, etc. Sometimes in working together one of us instructs or supervises the other. We make demands on each other: be on time for our meeting; do this task in this way; be careful with the record-player; don't leave the records on the floor.

Sometimes we are tired or lonely and we look for someone who will smile and be friendly while we rest or relax. Sometimes we find someone whose attitudes or thoughts challenge us, lead us along novel or adventurous paths. Sometimes we enjoy being quiet and want others to leave us alone.

Let us say that we find some or almost all of these behaviors in our interactions with most people.

How can we describe a relationship? How can we identify its most important aspects? Are there primary dimensions that matter most? Have these been identified by careful investigation and research?

THE BASIC DIMENSIONS OF A RELATIONSHIP

Think back over your interactions with others during the last day or two. What seems to impress you most about the way you and another person seem to get along, relate to each other, or feel about one another?

You will probably recall very easily that someone was angry with you or appeared to be. You will also quite readily recall if someone showed you kindness, tenderness, affection—especially if you felt yourself responding in a similar way. Thinking back, you may recall that someone tried to dominate you, demanded that you do something a certain way, tried to "push you around" or "put you down." You may, with some thought, remember someone who responded readily to your suggestions, seemed to want your advice, or tried to do things the way you like to see them done.

You may have difficulty recalling someone who seemed to be avoiding you or wanted to be left alone—they may have been so successful that you did not notice their avoidance behavior. However, on the other hand, you will likely recall with ease someone who seemed especially interested in talking with you, someone you were with a number of times during the day, a person with whom you interact frequently or for extended periods.

In the two preceding paragraphs we have suggested that there are different ways of relating to others. How many of these are really important or significant? In a particular relationship can these be identified and observed? Can the intensity of each be measured or estimated? If so, we may then be able to characterize a relationship and evaluate it along selected dimensions.

A rather large amount of research tends to support the conclusion that there are three primary dimensions in any human relationship. These are (1) the degree of *involvement*, (2) the amount of interpersonal *control*, and (3) *affect* or emotional tone—one's feelings. In his original attempt to identify these dimensions William Schutz summarized twenty years of research by students on the nature of human relationships.[1] He reviewed sixteen studies of parent-child relations, three analyses of "personality types" of interpersonal behavior, and ten major studies of interpersonal relations in groups. The findings of these studies all converge to support the conclusion that there are three basic dimensions: *involvement, control,* and *affect* or emotional tone. Each of these dimensions is different and distinct enough to be measured or estimated; together they cover the significant elements for describing a relationship. Schutz's own subsequent research has confirmed this conclusion.[2]

Interpersonal Involvement

The degree of involvement in a human relationship refers not only to the *amount* of interaction between the participants but also to the importance each attaches to this interaction. If two people seldom see or talk to each other, and when they do, simply exchange impersonal greetings, the degree of their mutual involvement with each other is small. This is especially true if they don't notice that for days they don't see each other. For example, you may have a classmate who ordinarily sits on the opposite side of the room. Did he attend class yesterday? If you can't remember, your degree of *involvement* in this relationship is low, even if you tend to see and talk to each other two or three times a week. Conversely, you and your father may live in different distant cities, see each other twice a year, and communicate only four or five times a year, and still have a high degree of *involvement* in your relationship. If each idea he presents, each sentence he speaks or writes, is given careful thought and attention, then your degree of *involvement* is high.

The degree of *involvement* is closely related to the amount of personal information exchanged. To be involved with someone you must know some things about him that matter to you, things that are significant.[3] If your *involvement* with another person is to be high, you and he will have to reveal significant parts of yourselves to each other. There are fairly dependable research data showing that when self-disclosure is high, interpersonal *involvement* is increased.[4]

Suppose, for example, that you meet someone on the tennis courts. You like his looks. This personal information initiates a degree of *involvement* on your part. You chat awhile and you like the sense of personal values implied by the conversation: he expresses loyalty to school, regard for friends, appreciation of personal skill and achievement. You play tennis for an hour and receive impressions of honesty in keeping score, determination to do one's best, fairness in judging out-of-bounds serves. At lunch you are impressed by his courtesy and consideration for others, cleanliness in eating habits, friendliness in meeting your needs or wishes. During the next half-hour you hear of his hopes for graduation, ambition to be a pediatrician, frustration over required courses, and sadness over the recent loss of a grandfather. If over the ensuing days such self-disclosure continues and you continue to be interested in such personal information, *involvement* in the relationship will increase. In addition, disclosure of the way he *feels about you* can lead to greater involvement.[5] If he shows you the way he feels regarding your hopes, ambitions, values and frustrations, your degree of *involvement* will be heightened, and the relationship will be of greater importance, both to you and to the other person.

As people interact and disclose items of personal information to each other they tend to reach little agreements on what is important and what is not. Out of this sharing comes a working consensus of mutual sympathy and consideration. There is also a tendency to close the gaps between their individual differences of opinion. In essence, *involvement* in a relationship means that participants interact in ways that are important to each other. As *involvement* is increased, the other two dimensions of a relationship become important: *control* and *affect* (emotional tone). In an established relationship the degree of involvement is usually quite stable. The amount of interaction may vary from day to day, but such variations are expected and routine. In such a relationship control and affect are of greatest concern.

The D-A-S-H Paradigm

In a relationship where involvement has become well established, the primary concerns will relate to control and affect. Interpersonal behavior related to *control* centers on who will make decisions and in what way. Positive control in a relationship is ordinarily referred to as dominance, influence, rule; use of power or authority; the role of superior, supervisor or leader. Negative control (or lack of it) in a relationship is ordinarily spoken of as submission, permissiveness or compliance; the role of follower.[6]

Behavior related to *affect* or emotional tone in a relationship involves expressions of warmth, acceptance and love, as well as hostility, rejection and hate. It is frequently characterized by such positive terms as "friendship," "emotionally close," "sweetheart," and such negative terms as "dislike," "coldness," and "anger."[7]

As noted earlier, *involvement* behavior is primarily concerned with inclusion of another person, the formation of a relationship. It focuses on degree of interaction and investment of time and energy with another person. Schutz noted this distinction thus: "Basically, inclusion is always concerned with whether or not a relation exists. Within existent relations, control is the area concerned with who gives orders and makes decisions for whom, whereas affection is concerned with how emotionally close or distant the relation becomes."[8]

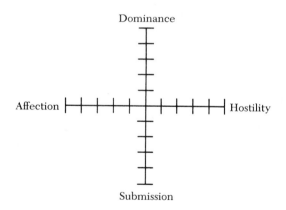

Figure 1

The D-A-S-H Paradigm of Interpersonal Relationships

The dimension of control may be characterized by a continuum; at one end is dominance and at the other is submission. The extent to which one person controls the other in the relationship may be described on a vertical line running between absolute dominance and abject submission (see figure 1). In like manner the dimension of *affect* or emotional tone may be characterized by a horizontal axis running between *affection* and *hostility*. Thus, the extent to which one person feels affection or hostility toward another in the relationship may be plotted along this horizontal line. Note that each of these basic dimensions of a relationship is bipolar and that each has a "zero" or neutral point in the center.

By way of illustration, your behavior toward another person in a relationship might be highly affectionate, or highly hostile, or somewhere between, including neutral—neither affectionate nor hostile. In addition, in this relationship you might be very dominant or very submissive or somewhere between, including neutral—neither dominant nor submissive.

In established relationships, such as those in families or work groups, these two basic dimensions, *dominance–submission* and *affection–hostility*, are the primary ones needed to describe the relationship. For example, the most significant aspects of the relationship between a father and his son, or a husband and wife, or a boss and secretary can be described on the D-A-S-H paradigm. A large number of fairly sophisticated studies, in attempting to identify significant elements in interpersonal relationships, support this point.

In an early (1957) study of relations between psychotherapists and their patients, Timothy Leary and his associates developed a framework for analyzing interpersonal behavior.[9] They identified two major factors: dominance–submission and hate–love. In addition, they represented variations of these elements on a wheel or "circumplex." The four quadrants of the wheel were divided into octants, and eight subcategories defined. The important thing about this circumplex formulation is that the subcategories were ordered in a circle, without severe breaks or any beginning or end. Thus, *all* interpersonal relationships are included. This formulation, in principle, has been supported in later studies. Although they used only rough empirical data, the intuition and insight of Leary and his associates seems to be quite remarkable in view of the findings of subsequent research.

In an early study of mother-child relations E. S. Schaefer identified two major factors: "control–autonomy" and "love–hostility."[10] In a review of other studies of child behavior Schaefer found the same two primary factors; in addition, the primary variables and intervariable relations formed a circumplex.[11] In a study of both mother and father behavior toward children Slater identified two similar factors: "Strictness–permissiveness" and "warmth–coldness."[12] Becker and his associates studied child behavior in relationships with parents and teachers, and found two basic factors: "extraversion–introversion" (containing a substantial dominance-submission component) and "emotional stability–instability" (containing a strong *hostile–nonhostile* component).[13] Following this study Becker and Krug compared data from six other studies, and two factors emerged: "assertiveness-submissiveness" and "loving-distrusting." Their intervariable correlations formed a circumplex.[14]

In a series of studies of college students in small problem-solving groups, Borgatta and his associates identified two basic dimensions of member relations: "individual assertiveness" and "sociability." Their relationship variations formed a circumplex.[15] An enlarged follow-up study by Borgatta found similar results.[16] A rather extensive series of studies of interpersonal behavior of adults by Lorr and McNair also identified two major variables: "dominance–submissiveness" and "affiliation–aggression," with fifteen intervariable behaviors forming a circumplex.[17]

In 1969 Robert Carson attempted to review all relevant studies of interpersonal relationships. His survey provided this summary:

> On the whole the conclusion seems justified that major portions of the domain of interpersonal behavior can profitably and reasonably accurately be conceived as involving variations on two independent bipolar dimensions. One of these may be called a *dominance–submission* dimension . . . The poles of the second principal dimension are perhaps best approximated by the terms *hate* versus *love*.[18]

It is of interest to compare these research findings with the results of scholarship in a related but entirely different area—that of psycholinguistics. Scholars in this area of investigation study the psychological implications of language usage. A well-known investigator in this area, Roger Brown, made very careful studies of words used by one person to address another, investigating such practices around the world. From these studies Brown concluded that forms of address "are always governed by the same two dimensions: solidarity and status." He further noted, "Solidarity and status appear to govern much of social life. They lie behind the great regulators of everyday behavior: the way in which similarity generates liking and interaction, which in turn produce more similarity; the way in which differential status confers power and privilege." There is little question that in essence Brown is here referring to the same two basic dimensions of interpersonal relations we have identified above: *affection–hostility* and *dominance–submission*. Brown concludes that these two factors permeate all human relationships and are obviously important "because we have all had to work them out in order to get along with others."[19]

The life-long work of Robert Bales should also be viewed in this context. For over twenty-five years he has been studying interpersonal behavior in various problem-solving or task-oriented groups.[20] In his extensive research he has identified three basic dimensions of interpersonal behavior: "up-down," associated with power and conformity; "positive-negative," associated with personal liking or group cohesiveness; and "forward-backward," a dimension less clearly defined, but generally related to progress in the problem-solving process. Obviously Bales' first two dimensions are very similar to those in our D-A-S-H paradigm: *dominance–submission* and *affection–hostility.* His third category, we believe, is a result of data derived entirely from *task-oriented* groups. It is reasonable to find in such groups considerable interpersonal behavior relating to progress in using the problem-solving process. This interpretation is in fact suggested by Bales: "The conceptual scheme of this book associates the forward direction (Forward–Backward Dimension) . . . with task orientation, that is, with task-seriousness. . . . It is assumed that the group to which the system is applied is in a task-oriented phase."[21] In essence, we believe that Bales' research supports our use of the D-A-S-H paradigm, and further suggests an additional dimension useful in analyzing relationships among members of problem-solving or task-oriented groups.

The D-A-S-H paradigm can be very valuable as a basic approach in analyzing our own personal relationships. It provides primary dimensions for our analysis. Instead of saying to ourselves, "I am usually quite friendly with Bob but he frequently makes me uncomfortable and I get angry," we can review our relationship with another person from a broad perspective. We can ask, where do we stand on dominance–submission and affection–hostility. Are we generally dominant or submissive? Are we usually affectionate or hostile? In this fashion we can arrive at a fairly comprehensive summary of our relationship. We do so by looking backward and reviewing significant events and behaviors in our relationship. In addition, we observe more carefully interaction events as they occur today and in ensuing days. We note evidence pro and con our tentative conclusions regarding our relationship. We note especially a friendly smile, our smile unreturned, a warm handclasp, a frown, "hard looks," and other such behaviors that Erving Goffman calls "tie-signs,"[22] indications that the relationship is generally affectionate or hostile. We also note with greater care indications that we (or they) are being dominated, manipulated, influenced or "pushed around."

The D-A-S-H paradigm can be very useful to you as you attempt to summarize your relationship with another person. The *essential character* of any relationship can be graphed on this model. For example, relationships between you (Y) and another person (P) might be summarized in one of the ways shown in figure 2. Note that the degree of dominance, affection, submission, or hostility of each person is shown by the distance of Y or P from the center of the D-A-S-H axes.

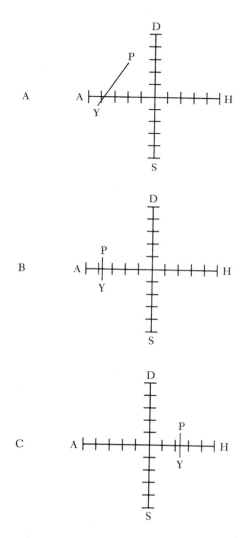

Figure 2
Examples of Possible Interpersonal Relationships

As you have been looking over these pages, very likely you have been thinking about one of your own interpersonal relationships. Perhaps it is the one you have with your father. You might conclude, after giving it some thought, that this relationship resembles the one described in figure 2–B, involving considerable affection on the part of both of you, but containing some dominating behavior by your father to which you respond with small tokens of submission. If you are just now entering adult life, it is quite possible that 2–C may more accurately describe the current power-struggle and attendant emotional feelings between you and your father.

To properly use the D-A-S-H model you should think carefully about your relationship with another person. Graph it as best you can. Reflect for awhile; compare this relationship with others in which you are currently involved. Also compare it with relationships between other people you know. Review your plot on the graph and change it as seems reasonable. Then pay special attention to events that transpire over a number of days. See if your tentative summary of the relationship seems to be supported; if not, change it to comply with your observations.

We have previously suggested that, to evaluate a relationship, we must first analyze it. Analysis can be implemented by use of the D-A-S-H paradigm. We can further illustrate this procedure by consideration of a selected interpersonal relationship. In his book, *Games People Play*, Eric Berne has described numerous interaction behaviors. Let us consider the interaction in the game he calls "Corner." Essentially it consists of a delayed refusal to follow the other person's ploy to get you to show affection. A wife suggests to her husband that they go to a movie; he agrees. All is well so far. They could be happy going off together to the movie. Now, however, comes the ploy: she makes an "unthinking" suggestion that maybe they shouldn't spend the money "because the house needs painting." He has previously told her that they don't have the money to paint the house "just now." Therefore, he doesn't see this as a "reasonable" comparison between such an expensive operation and the price of a movie. And here comes his delayed refusal to follow her ploy. He responds rudely to her remark. He knows very well from past experience that he should not take her "house-painting" remark seriously. He knows that what she really wants is to be reassured, told that everything will come out all right, be "honeyed-up" a bit. But he has refused to go this route, and gives his wife rudeness. She is now "offended" and says that since he is in a bad mood, she will not go to the movie with him and in her desire to give him a "put down," *suggests that he go alone.* This is the critical ploy of the game. He must now leap over two hurdles (two ploys) to give her the desired affection; if he did so, they could still have a happy movie together. But he has been put down pretty hard. To resurrect his pride, he must act as if her "put down" didn't hurt him; so here comes the final ploy of the game. He refuses to give her reassurance and affection (one wonders how he possibly could at this stage) and he leaves, looking abused but perhaps secretly feeling relieved. She is left feeling resentful. Who "won" this game? Did the husband, since all he did was follow her suggestion—literally? Berne's conclusion is, "They both knew this is cheating, but since she said it, she *is cornered.*"[23]

The "cornering" game is a fairly complicated social maneuver. Instead of her making a forthright request for reassurance, she provides two consecutive unrealistic *hurdles* over which her husband must jump before he can give her what she wants. Of course, if he *did* cross these in order to reach her and meet her needs, she could be pretty certain that he really cares about her. With some experience he will come to recognize her attempts to make him jump hurdles as efforts to manipulate his behavior, strategies to maneuver him into a "show" of affection whether he feels it or not. Eventually he will recognize it for what it is, an effort to *control* his behavior, an issue of dominance–submission, an incipient power-play, with no real affection involved. In time, he is likely to view such strategies as essentially hostile and seek ways to defend himself, counteracting it with hostile behavior of his own. In passing, we should note the "sick" aspect—the unsatisfying, self-defeating quality—of forced or manipulated displays of affection.

If playing such games were the standard interaction for two persons, their relationship would have to be plotted in the dominant–hostile quadrant of the D-A-S-H model, with both persons' behavior represented as *dominant* in nature (even though not always highly successful) and both quite *hostile.*

It is extremely interesting to read Berne's analysis of games that people sometimes play. It is even more interesting to plot such players' relationships on the D-A-S-H model. In many cases these efforts give deeper insights into the realities of the described relationship. What the players are doing to each other is just as interesting as how they play. In some cases we have gained greater insight into our own interpersonal behavior and the implications of strategies we have caught ourselves trying to use.

THE RELATIONSHIP DIMENSIONS IN ACTION

As you interact with another person certain things happen to your relationship that can be explained, and to some extent predicted, by the D-A-S-H paradigm. Let's suppose that you are a young woman and you meet a man you have not met before. As you are introduced and start to get acquainted you find him quite attractive. You also sense that he shows warmth and friendliness—even potential affection. In addition you note that he tends to dominate your conversation and insists that he take you to lunch. If you stop to think about it, you realize that his interpersonal behavior toward you can be identified as falling somewhere in the dominant–affectionate quadrant. Let us further suppose that your recent experiences with male friends have produced in you a need to resist being led or pushed, and that you are not about to let it happen again, particularly with a new acquaintance. On the other hand, let us suppose that your efforts at resistance of domination have somewhat cooled your relations with other young men, and that at this time you feel warmly appreciative of signs of potential male friendliness and affection.

We can tentatively predict that you and your new acquaintance will engage in a fairly friendly power struggle. In addition, you will be somewhat torn between wanting to accept his friendly attention and resisting his domination. You may, for example, insist on paying for your own lunch but hope he will ask you to dinner. Your power struggle may soon terminate the relationship; either he or you may tire of the required effort and you may not bother with each other further. Or the friendly warmth and potential affection may keep the relationship going; the two of you may find ways of sharing power or influence over each other. Perhaps you may allow yourself to be dominated only in small ways that do not appear to be very important.

Note that we have said little about where you go together or what you do. You may work together, eat together, exchange personal views and ideas. These things, of course, matter. But we are suggesting that what matters most to you in a relationship with another person are the degrees of domination of one over the other and the emotional tone of your feelings toward each other—the degrees of dominance–submission and affection–hostility.

Affection and Hostility Elicit Similar Responses

In a relationship affectionate behavior on the part of one person tends to produce affectionate responses on the part of the other; on the other hand, hostile behavior tends to produce hostility. Behavior that can be characterized as severe hostility nearly always produces resentment, dislike, and anger; over time, many people learn to hate. We may thus conclude that *interpersonal behavior characterized along the bipolar dimension of affection-hostility ordinarily elicits similar responses.*[24]

Dominance and Submission Elicit Reciprocal Responses

Dominant behavior in a relationship tends to produce submissive responses; this, of course, is only true if interaction continues.[25] If dominant behavior by one person is continued and resistance is shown by the other person, the relationship may very likely be terminated, sometimes before it gets started. If a relationship is continued in which a power-struggle occurs, this struggle may last for days, months, or even years. In some families it may never be resolved; it may lead to use of manipulative games or strategies that continue endlessly.[26] Concerning power, it is interesting to note that while the appetite for sex or comfort is limited, the appetite for power can be limitless.[27]

Submissive behavior in a relationship tends to elicit domination by the other person.[28] If you are dominated, it is not entirely the other person's fault. Submission reinforces dominating behavior, and vice versa. We may thus state a second principle of interpersonal behavior in action: *behavior that may be characterized along the bipolar dimension of dominance–submission tends to elicit reciprocal behavior; dominance reinforces submission; submission reinforces dominance.*[29]

Let's turn our attention once again to the imaginary relationship previously discussed: you a young woman, warmly interacting with a young man who attempts to dominate you in a friendly way. Let us suppose that the interpersonal warmth continues and the attempts to dominate largely subside. The relationship might then be graphed on the D-A-S-H paradigm as illustrated in figure 3. As you and he interact, your interpersonal behavior as well as his can largely be explained and predicted in terms of the two principles cited above: affection or hostility tend to elicit *similar* responses, and dominance or submissiveness tend to elicit *reciprocal* responses. As you and he continue to interact, your behavior produces responses by him; these responses in turn produce responses by you.

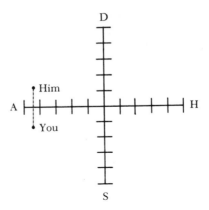

Figure 3.
A Warm Relationship with a Small Amount of Dominance and
Submission

The "Lock-Step" Effect

Responses produce responses that produce responses. As you continue to interact with another person, the two of you tend to work
out a "shared definition" of your relationship.[30] In some relationships
the original "starting" behavior and early response series may be
forgotten; in some cases it may have never consciously been perceived or noticed; in other cases it may have been misperceived
because of anticipated behavior or responses that never actually
materialized. However, once the chain of response to response to
response to behavior has been set in motion, these responses to
responses tend to produce what may be called a "lock-step" effect.
Once a "lock-step" has become established, it is very difficult to
break. This *tendency to respond automatically*, almost without
thinking, in terms of behavior that is dominant or submissive and
affectionate or hostile is a principle of human relationships early
identified by Leary and his associates. Leary called this phenomenon
the "interpersonal reflex."[31]

The Interpersonal Response Repertoire

Some people appear to have a narrow or rigid orientation to all or
nearly all other people. They tend to respond to nearly all others in
about the same way. Not unusually this narrow response repertoire

will consist of hostile-submissive behavior. Such responses, repeatedly given, tend to elicit a singular hostile–dominant response from others, and a rather unsatisfying lock-step goes into full swing.

On the other hand, many persons have a wider repertoire of responses, and can appropriately react in different ways to differing interpersonal behaviors of others. *The range of a person's response repertoire tends to determine the degree of rigidity of his or her interpersonal relationships as well as the degree of satisfaction that can be derived from them.* A person who relates well with others tends to use a wide range of responses in various different interpersonal situations.[32]

A person with a narrow interpersonal response repertoire is often in trouble. In cases where his repertoire is extremely narrow his behavior frequently takes the form of showing fear of all people. This person in ordinary social settings will be notably dysfunctional and often identified as "mentally ill."[33]

Less extreme forms of a narrow interpersonal response repertoire very often occur. You may have met people and called them "one-way." Not infrequently "one-way" people respond to nearly all other people by trying to dominate them while at the same time showing a superficial manipulative friendliness. Such people, of course, are not totally limited in their interpersonal relationships—just narrow in their response repertoire. An example of a limited repertoire is the "no alternative" person. He may say, "I had no alternative but to fire him," or "She left me no alternative." He often views other persons as "things" to be used or manipulated.[34]

On rare occasions two people, each having narrow response repertoires, may succeed in establishing a relationship if the two repertoires are congenial. In this relationship one can expect to find a very high degree of rigidity and a notable example of "lock-step" behavior.

One of the major purposes of an encounter group or laboratory training group in human relations is to determine the extent of your interpersonal response repertoire. Do you tend to respond in the same way to all group members when they talk to you in different ways? For example, are you always defensive? Do you act toward all people as if they are trying to manipulate or influence you? If some group member shows you friendliness and potential regard or affection, do you show suspicion and hostile resistance? These are very important questions to consider as you attempt to evaluate your ways of relating to other persons.

We are not always aware of how we are behaving; we actually may be *dominating* another person when we fully believe all we are doing is making sure they have sufficient relevant *facts*. Additionally we are not fully aware of how another person is *perceiving* our behavior unless he gives us adequate verbal or nonverbal feedback. A primary purpose of encounter groups and human relations training is to give us feedback on our interpersonal behavior as it is perceived by others.

EVALUATING A RELATIONSHIP

As we pointed out in the early part of this chapter, in order to evaluate a relationship we must first analyze it. We have shown how this can be done by summarizing it on the D-A-S-H dimensions. After this is done, we can proceed to evaluate it according to (1) how it meets our interpersonal needs and (2) what kinds of alternative relationships appear to be available to us.

Comparing Our Needs with Rewards Received

As you compare your interpersonal needs with the conditions in an existing relationship, the issue is simply stated: Are you happy with what you have? Are your needs being met? Only you can decide what is satisfying to you. Your needs will not necessarily be like those of most other people. You may, as an individual, feel a need to be dominated, told what to do; you may be convinced that without such direction from another person your life is too puzzling, that its problems overwhelm you. On the other hand, you personally may not have any such need at all.

We have indicated in chapter three that the interpersonal needs most commonly identified through research are (1) *inclusion* in interactions with others, (2) an agreement on who is *controlling* whom under various conditions, and (3) demonstrations of *warmth* or affection. As you can see, these needs are closely related to the significant dimensions of a relationship included in our D-A-S-H paradigm; in addition, the dimension of *inclusion* relates to the process by which a relationship becomes established.

As you compare your own needs with the benefits received from a particular relationship, you employ a specific procedure that we have earlier identified as calculating the cost/reward ratio of the relationship. This process has been discussed by psychologists as a theory of interaction outcomes, as well as a theory of social exchange. The two theories agree remarkably in essential principles although differing somewhat in minor details.[35]

A relationship may be rewarding in terms of satisfying our interpersonal needs for inclusion, affection and/or control. Costs consist of investments of time and energy. Considerable energy can be expended in feelings of anxiety, anger, or embarrassment; punishment of either a physical or psychological nature can have high cost-value.

When we make initial contact with another person establishing a relationship will largely depend upon the cost/reward ratio for either them or us. In our early contacts we tend to explore relationship possibilities. Over a period of time we arrive at a general evaluation of the relationship. Behaviors that are rewarded are repeated. Costly behaviors are avoided. If a relationship becomes rather costly to us, we tend to discontinue the interaction. George C. Homans, a well-known student of this process, explained it in terms of the "principle of distributive justice"—we don't like to give more than we receive.[36]

Assessing Available Alternative Relationships

As we compare the costs of a relationship with its rewards, we also compare this ratio with estimates of the potential of other relationships available to us. We seek an answer to this question: Can we spend available time and energy in a more satisfying relationship with some other person or persons?[37] If our answer seems to be in the affirmative, we pursue a new relationship and let the less satisfying one die or deteriorate into an acquaintanceship with little involvement.

Before we decide to terminate a relationship we should consider very carefully the *degree* of our various interpersonal needs and the cost we are willing to pay to have these needs met by others. Are we expecting too much for what we are willing to give? Taking advantage of available alternatives may require that we change some of our ways of interacting. For example, we may have to give up the habit of trying to dominate others. If available *alternative* relationships require a change on our part, what might such a change produce *in the relationship we already have?*

In seeking answers to the questions posed above, we usually need to take a very careful look at ourselves. Participation in an encounter group in which we obtain reliable feedback from others can often help us to see ourselves better. As we struggle to deal with these questions, it may be helpful to focus upon special problems that ordinarily arise as one person attempts to develop a satisfactory relationship with another. The nature of such frequently encountered problems is the subject of our next chapter.

SUMMARY

In this chapter we have attempted to present procedures for analyzing and evaluating an interpersonal relationship. We have suggested that involvement in the interaction of another is necessary for a relationship to become established. Involvement can refer both to the amount of interaction and to its significance to the persons involved. Self-disclosure is recognized as a primary means of making interaction significant in a relationship.

We have cited considerable research findings to show that in an established relationship there are two significant dimensions of interpersonal behavior: dominance–submission and affection–hostility. We have displayed this relationship paradigm in the form of a D-A-S-H model. In addition, we have noted that affectionate and hostile behaviors tend to elicit *similar* behaviors in response: affection tends to produce affection and hostility tends to produce hostility. On the other hand, dominance and submission tend to produce their *reciprocals:* dominance (if the relationship survives) tends to produce submission, and submission tends to produce dominance.

When such behaviors occur in a relationship responses tend to produce responses that produce responses in line with the principles of similarity and reciprocity outlined above. As the response to response to response to behavior becomes established, a "lock-step" pattern develops in the relationship; this "lock-step" chain is usually very hard to break.

We have further suggested that the degree to which an individual can respond to others in various different ways may be viewed as his interpersonal response repertoire. If this repertoire is limited or very narrow, he will find others responding to him in essentially the same way, based upon the principles of similarity and reciprocity suggested above. His own response to others may at times not be very appropriate, but more often than not *their* responses to him will be appropriate but limited in range because of the narrowness of his response repertoire. If he gives others little to work with he will get a narrow range of responses in return.

We have suggested that the above concepts may be used to analyze one's own interpersonal relationships. Once analyzed, they may be evaluated in terms of the degree to which they meet one's interpersonal needs. Although as individuals our needs will not be the same as those of many other individuals, people in general have interpersonal needs for inclusion, affection, and control (both of and by themselves). Analysis of a relationship using the D-A-S-H paradigm can facilitate assessment of its value in meeting one's needs for inclusion, affection, and control. Further evaluation can be achieved by comparing these benefits with our personal costs of time and energy invested in the relationship. Final evaluation may be achieved by comparing the cost/reward ratio thus derived with estimates of the potential cost/reward ratio of other relationships available to us.

Encounter groups and other types of training in human relations can help us to see ourselves better. We can, by participating with others and then obtaining their perceptions of us, obtain a better view of our own interpersonal response repertoire. In addition we may be able to make better judgments about the costs we ought to be willing to bear in order to have our interpersonal needs met by others.

5

bAsic pRoblems iN
tHe lAboRAtoRy gRoup

In a very real sense every group experience is a unique adventure. Just as every human is a distinct, differentiated individual, so too are groups different. Up to this point we have been generalizing on processes that tend to make a group function successfully. This chapter will analyze the causes and symptoms of some common problems that may interfere with group growth and development, and describe some methods of diagnosis. The four problem areas that we will discuss are: (1) distrust and defensiveness; (2) lack of cohesion and group compatibility; (3) handling of power and control; and (4) phases in group development.

DISTRUST AND DEFENSIVENESS

Perhaps it would be helpful initially to look at group behaviors in terms of a continuum of climates. At one end we would have a defensive climate and at the other what we will label an "accepting." open climate. In chapter three we discussed how we develop trust by tossing out pieces of ourselves to the group and then testing their reactions. If we get a "wrong" response then we establish our "trust limit" and refrain from disclosing more of ourselves to the group.

In a defensive climate we are unwilling to share ourselves or to trust things about ourselves with others. Conversely, in an open climate, to the extent that people can free their time, energies, and emotions used to protect themselves from others, they can experience real freedom of action and release their energies toward productive, creative endeavors.

In chapter two we discussed the importance of self-esteem in the individual. It is now pertinent to examine the role of defensiveness in maintaining self-esteem. Defensiveness has been termed a "compensation" because of its technique of "adding to" or "detracting from" so as to achieve a balanced stability within the self. According to Argyris, the individual's degree of defensiveness will determine how he will perceive received feedback.[1] The person's initial feelings of defensiveness when faced with a threatening situation will greatly alter perceptions he makes. These altered perceptions might easily result in a projection of hostile feelings toward other members of the group. Feshback and Singer report on a study of the effects of fear arousal and suppression of fear upon social perception. Subjects exposed to a fear-producing situation perceived the stimulus person as significantly more fearful and more aggressive than did the control groups.[2] This generally supports Argyris' theory that a person's degree of defensiveness in a situation will determine how he perceives the other individuals in the situation and the entire situation itself (this might also be true in reverse).

Therefore, besides perceptual differences, a *communication* problem also exists in a climate of defensive behavior. Although most people can tolerate different opinions in subjective matters, little toleration exists for someone who differs with them on some matter perceived as "reality" to them, e.g. music, religion, politics. When both people perceive the matter as having different objective "reality" they are no longer arguing about that reality as much as they are arguing about themselves and their individual experiences.[3]

As we noted, Argyris upholds self-acceptance as one of a person's most basic needs, and that his degree of defensiveness will guard him against negative feedback that might threaten to damage his self-acceptance. Moreover, Argyris suggests that individuals become more accepting of themselves through successful interpersonal relationships, which are, he postulates, "the source of psychological life and growth."[4] Piaget's thoughts concur with this theory: "It is only through constant dialogue with others that we can get a perspective of ourselves and get an understanding of any permanence of concepts."[5] It would seem then that the defensive person is in a double bind—if a person is defensive, he will discount any evaluative feedback and be very limited in his trust and acceptance of others (which are necessary for the authentic relationship of which Argyris speaks) yet it is these successful relationships that he must reach for in order to increase his self-acceptance.

Another concept intricately woven into the defense phenomenon is interpersonal trust. It is reasonable to connect lack of defensiveness toward another as a possible index of the degrees of trust held in that person. Morton Deutsch's work is concerned with how trust is affected by an individual's perception of the intentions of the other person. He found that individuals who were trusting and trustworthy expected others to be the same.[6] People low in defensiveness consider themselves as trusting and trustworthy and see others as acting the same. It appears then that lack of trust is a prominent factor within defensive behavior. Deutsch also saw three types of motivational orientations within interpersonal interactions:

(A) Cooperative—where the welfare of both participants is of mutual concern.

(B) Individualistic—where both participants are out for self, but no actual cost is required of other.

(C) Competitive—where both participants are out for self at the expense of the other.

He reasons that when the interaction is perceived as a cooperative one, both parties will be more trusting and trustworthy (and thereby less defensive). To a degree, therefore, defensiveness is but a façade presented both to protect a person's self-image and to grant that person the supportive acceptance by others which he assumes would not be granted were he to be completely open with his feelings and attitudes.

Goffman deals with another concept related to defensiveness—"wrong face" and "out of face." I am in "wrong face" when I cannot integrate some information about my social self into either my self-image or my self as seen by others. Moreover, I am said to be "out of face" when I am not ready with appropriate behavior (words or actions) that a group expects. Goffman also notes that when a person feels "in face" he will respond with confidence and assurance, and conversely, when he is in "wrong face" or "out of face," he feels ashamed, inferior, and threatened. People's ability to cover this embarrassment in themselves is referred to as "poise" by Goffman.[7]

A strong tendency exists in groups to keep a certain level of consideration for persons temporarily in wrong face or out of face, i.e. to go to lengths to save the feelings and face of others. Although perhaps partially stemming from the group's wish to protect members, a group also wants to avoid the experience of uneasiness and embarrassment when one of its members is embarrassed. Some of these protective maneuvers include pretending that no threat to face has occurred. Thus, for example, a man whose stomach growls may not acknowledge that it was he, and the group, through "tactful blindness," also does not "hear" the noise. When a person is unexpectedly caught "out of face" the other members may ignore him for a moment so that he may reassemble himself.[8] Those protective maneuvers are welcomed when one's stomach growls, but if they extend to a mutual overlooking of everything, the acceptance is not actually a real and open one, and thus is not serviceable to a successful relationship.

Recognizing all the aspects of defensiveness that are barriers to effective communication, the problem of how to cope with (not eliminate) defensiveness arises. Argyris reasons that a way to lessen the occurrences of defensiveness is to give feedback that "describes a relationship without placing a value judgment on it."[9] In this way the individual receives the open feedback necessary for an effective relationship, yet he feels neither threatened nor does he feel the need to act defensively.

However, in order for this initial interaction of nonevaluative, but descriptive, feedback to take place, the sender (S) must be nondefensive if he is to send nondistorted feedback to the receiver (R). R must develop a degree of trust toward S so that he can accept the feedback nondefensively. Consequently a "human bind" exists and *any* defensive behavior may circulate and create similar defensiveness in the other person.

Jack Gibb has suggested that a "supportive atmosphere" should pervade. He lists two sets of behavioral climates (in small groups). One set arouses defensiveness (left-hand column) because of the threat of being watched by a "secretive dogmatic judge" who has no concern for the individual within the group. The other set reduces defensiveness (right-hand column) by offsetting this defensive atmosphere with a more objective, yet supportive, outlook.[10]

1. Evaluation	1. Description
2. Control	2. Problem Orientation
3. Strategy	3. Spontaneity
4. Neutrality	4. Empathy
5. Superiority	5. Equality
6. Certainty	6. Provisionalism

Although these supportive categories are helpful, a completely supportive climate is often more complex than these six behaviors would indicate. All of these behaviors are perceived, but a defensive person will be less able to perceive accurately. In this respect, Carl Rogers speaks of the need to be "open" to experience in order to evaluate threat more accurately and be able to tolerate change more easily.[11] The degree to which a group climate can approach being called supportive, then, will initially depend on the individuals' level of defensiveness as well as the overall attitudes of the group at the time.[12] However, within this circular interaction it is reasonable to be able to diminish gradually the individual's feelings of threat by creating trust and more cohesiveness in the group's attitudes. These feelings of trust and cohesiveness could be well-implemented by initiating Gibb's "supportive behaviors" within the group setting.

LACK OF COHESION AND GROUP COMPATIBILITY

The growth of a sense of "groupness" occurs in laboratory groups. After the group has gone through a period of expressed expectations, fears, and personal feelings of threat, distinct feelings and concerns for the group as a whole should develop. Statements such as, "Will this be best for the group?" and "What does the group think?" reflect this concern. This feeling of groupness has been labeled "cohesiveness."

The need to belong to the group can be perverted in laboratory training groups in the academic setting. Within a structured setting, including specific length of meeting times, textbooks, grades, and exams, the group experience can pose special problems with members' desires toward the experience. Some members may join the group as a major requirement or for other academic need. These members may feel that their only attraction to the group is the academic necessity. This can lead to an avoidance of vital group functioning resulting in a lowering of group cohesiveness. However, each member must assess for himself what his needs in the group are, and what he expects to receive from the group experience. This degree of need is central to the development of group attraction and resultant cohesiveness.

James Dittes, in a study of college freshmen, arrived at four specific factors which correlate individual need and group attraction and cohesiveness:

1. If a person has a relatively strong need, his attraction to the group is likely to vary directly with the extent to which the group satisfies that need.
2. If an individual's need is low, the degree of gratification afforded by the group is a relatively less important determinant of attraction. In the extreme case of a person with a need at zero level, the amount of potential gratification or frustration of that need by the group has no effect on his level of attraction toward the group.
3. If a group offers relatively great satisfaction of a particular need, a person's attraction to the group should vary directly with the strength of that need.
4. If a group definitely frustrates a need, attraction should vary inversely with the strength of the need. A person with a stronger need should experience greater punishment in the frustration and consequently reduce his attraction toward the group by the greatest amount. If attraction in any instance were dependent solely on this single need, its frustration would drive an individual to leave the group. In most instances, attraction depends on many other factors and may remain positive, even though sharply reduced by the frustration of a strong need.[13]

It appears that much of Dittes' theory can be applied to the laboratory training group experience. At times a person may seek a T-group experience, desiring a high degree of concern for his individual problems. This group experience can have two different outcomes that are directly related to the individual's perceptions. If the individual feels that his needs have been satisfied, then it is likely that he will feel close to the group. On the other hand, if the individual feels that the group has not dealt with his problems, his conception might be that the group is useless. He might also take the position that if the group cannot be of help, it is worthless to become an integral member. Cases such as this seem to be an important part of the establishment of group cohesiveness. The development of cohesiveness must rest with each individual, and the loss of a single member greatly reduces the entire functioning of the group as a whole.

In much the same way, a person without any perceived need would not be affected by direct group concern for his needs. In general, the perceived needs of membership that we discussed in chapter two seem to be an integral part of the formation of group cohesiveness. Not only are the perceived needs important, but also the perceived gain. If a person feels great satisfaction of a particular need then his desired membership in the group should be advanced.

Dittes' fourth point concerning frustration of need seems applicable to laboratory training groups in that individual needs must be dealt with if the entire group is to function. If the group frustrates a need by overlooking it, the resultant behavior of the individual involved might be withdrawal or expressed animosity toward the group. When the group is not living up to an individual's expectations it would seem that the natural behavior would be for that person to take less credence in the activities of the group. Conversely, when an individual perceives himself as being helped by membership in the group, his attraction increases.

Ewart Smith has stated that "the time and energy used by group members in attempting to predict the behavior of others reduces the amount of group energy available for any given goal or task."[14] If this is the case, the development of group cohesiveness would be unattainable. It seems that an attempt to predict the behavior of members is a continuing pattern in T-group development. Although this may not always be the most positive avenue, it certainly is a central part of much of the group experience. As members probe for behavioral patterns they are also searching for a reduction of personal threat and frustration which can be a factor in the development of a cohesive group. It appears that the time spent in groups searching for the behavioral patterns of other members contributes to the development of a cohesive group.

The group's cohesiveness is directly related to three issues to be confronted by each group member:

1. *Investment*—"How much of myself—time, energy, resources— must I give in order to gain needed cooperation to achieve my goals?" As we discussed in chapter four, the cost/reward ratio is constantly being considered as each individual attempts to determine if personal goals can be achieved without the group's cooperation and, "What is the *most* that such cooperation is likely to cost me?"

2. *Compatibility*—"Are their goals compatible with mine?" Each individual attempts to determine if he wishes to accomplish the same ends as the group, whether the value systems are approximately the same, and whether differences in the group truly make any difference.

3. *Satisfaction*—"How valuable are the relationships in the group to me?" The degree of the reward is matched against costs and the individual determines, "How many of my goals am I accomplishing (or likely to achieve)?"

HANDLING OF POWER AND CONTROL

A third issue which a new member faces, and which must be resolved in any new group, is the distribution of power and influence. It can be safely assumed that every member will have some need to control and influence others, but the amount of this need and its form of expression will vary from person to person. One member may wish to influence the methods used by the group, another may wish to influence the agenda or goals, while a third may wish to achieve an overall position of prominence in the group. The dilemma for all members early in the group's history is that they do not know each other's needs or styles, and hence cannot easily determine who will be able to influence whom and what.

When discussing control, one has many components to identify and evaluate. Some of these definitions are obvious in their descriptions, others are not central or important in relationship to the laboratory training group. Control based on physical threat, implied or overt, is not of concern in this chapter for it has very little relevance to the T-group. Control based on the exercise of punishment such as laws, statutes, constitutions, and written rules is similarly not central to the T-group. Control through societal norms and group pressure; control through positive reinforcement and control through psychological constraints, such as withholding love, affection, or inclusion; all are involved in the laboratory training group process.

Control through Societal Norms and Group Pressure

Asch's conformity studies have defined for us control through group pressure.[15] The object of the studies was to investigate the social and personal conditions that induce individuals to resist or to yield to group pressures when the latter are perceived to be contrary to fact.

The experimenters placed an individual in a relationship of conflict with all members of a group of eight. The subject was submitted to two contradictory forces, his own experience and perception of the length of a line and the unanimous evidence of the group of equals. The results showed that one-third placed their estimate with the group. One-fourth of the subjects stayed with their own perceptions, and the remainder vacillated between the group and their own perceptions. They also found that the majority effect grew stronger as the situation diminished in clarity. Independence and yielding appeared to be joint functions of the character of the stimulus situation, the clarity of the stimuli; the character of group forces; the amount of unanimity of opinion; and the character of the individual. All of this has relevance for us when we look at the group pressure in the T-group as a form of control and manipulation.

Bettelheim, in an article based on his prisoner of war experience at Dachau and Buchenwald in 1938–39, showed the effect of group pressure on establishment of social order.[16] The group pressures of the old prisoners to make the new prisoners conform was the social order in the camp. The pressures were such that one denied self and dignity to conform and often regressed to childlike behavior in order to fit the order established by the old prisoners. This serves as an example of how strong and powerful the group pressure can be, even to the exclusion of man's other needs and survival.

Control through Positive Reinforcement

People tend to respond in blind faith to reward, to promises, and to reassurances. This is called reward conditioning. We have been reinforced in our behavior since we were infants. Most of our public education and childhood training is based on reinforcement theory. A good grade, a loving gesture, a position converted are all rewards for acceptable behavior but are also forms of control centered in the parent or the teacher. The decision must be made at some point about which behavior is rewarded. Inherent in that decision is a form of control. Therefore the *control through positive reinforcement* is accomplished by reinforcing behavior someone decides should be rewarded and thereby reinforced.

The famous Skinner-Rogers debate of *Walden Two* versus *Client-centered Therapy* focused on the "control" dilemma posed by reinforcement theory.[17] B. F. Skinner, a psychologist who developed many of our ideas about reinforcement and learning theory, saw reinforcement as a force mainly for good; Rogers claimed that any form of control or manipulation was negative. Skinner felt that fear of control leads to a misinterpretation of valid practices and a blind rejection of planning. He argued that effective behavior change inevitably involves some degree of control or manipulation, and this change should be based on intelligent planning and positive reinforcement. Most of the techniques of control are so ingrained in our culture that we cannot view them as manipulative. Skinner's point was that control is so much a part of our everyday experience that the evaluation should not be in the use of control or reinforcement to gain certain ends, but in the goal or end product itself. Skinner's points are summarized in a conversation in *Walden Two* between Mr. Castle and Frazier.

"No, Mr. Castle, there's no alternative to a planned society. We can't leave mankind to an accidental or biased control. But by using the principle of positive reinforcement—carefully avoiding force or the threat of force—we can preserve a personal sense of freedom."[18]

Carl Rogers' answers revolve around the personal view that any control impinges on man's autonomy. Rogers argues that intelligent planning and positive reinforcement involve goal setting for someone else. The setting of these goals is the choice of the reinforcer and contains his values, thus he is controlling or manipulating the one he is reinforcing. Rogers says that when one talks about control in this sense he must ask, "Who will be controlled?" "Who will exercise the control?" and that involves one individual controlling the other. If one makes the value decision on the basis of the end product or the purpose of the reinforcement, Rogers argues that one must pick values that may not always be positive to each person. Rogers places acceptance of the other at the center of his methodology and lets the client make the choice of the goals for himself. The teacher or the therapist only reflects, listens, and empathizes.

Control through Psychological Constraints

In chapter four we cited the view of William Schutz on the role of control in the decision-making relationship between people. He sees control with interactional qualities. He states that all people have needs for and desires to control, and feels control is basic to people in that it is part of all interpersonal relationships. Finding mutual compatibility in the area of control is a frequent task of a group. The interactional qualities of control, the functional need states of control, and finding compatibility in control provide us with a framework to look at control and its qualities in the T-group. There are several characteristics of a T-group that make it especially suited for exploitive use of control: the nature of a small informal group; the emphasis on cohesion; the emphasis on self-disclosure and openness; the use of feedback; the pressure on the deviant.

Since control and manipulation are inevitable in a T-group setting, a certain degree of control will be exercised in any situation. The key seems to be in its recognition and use. Understanding the dynamics of control increases our awareness. To evaluate its use we suggest using the goal of enhancement of each individual's areas of choice. Kelman suggests some criteria to use in its evaluation.[19] To what extent does the discussion allow for or enhance the person's freedom of choice, to what extent is the relationship reciprocal, to what extent is the situation oriented toward the welfare of the one receiving feedback rather than the one giving it? Leonard Krasner stated: "To recognize and be aware of the influence of control represents freedom and responsibility in its finest sense: to deny it—represents shirking of responsibility and a genuine loss of freedom."[20]

As a guide to increasing our awareness of control, and to enhance the freedom of choice in the T-group, we suggest:

1. Many of the principles of group dynamics are based on democratic values. They are designed to involve the individual in the decision-making process and to foster self-expression on the part of the individual member. Continued practice in the decision-making process can increase one's understanding of the dynamics of control.

2. The T-group process should increase the individual's awareness of control and should raise some of the ethical issues inherent in control.

3. The enhancement of freedom of choice should be a goal of the T-group. The learning experience would be the broadening of one's areas of choices. A person's sharing would involve widening the other's areas of choice.

4. Feedback should be a mutual influence attempt always involving interaction between members. The individual should learn to recognize and label feedback as laden with the individual's perceptions and values. The individual seeking feedback should be allowed to set the structure and determine the direction of feedback.

5. Less emphasis should be placed on cohesion, and if cohesion is set as a goal the group should be aware of the "costs" of cohesiveness.

6. The potential (both positive and negative) of social pressure, reinforcement, defense mechanisms, self-disclosure, and openness

should be explored in the T-group. Additionally self-disclosure should be voluntary and guided and controlled by each individual.

7. The group should be prepared to protect the individual member from subtle pressures exerted by the group to force the "deviant" member to conform. Each member should recognize the other members' rights to withdraw from any activity at any time.

Bennis and Shepard, in developing a theory of group development, point appropriately to the problems of power and control as key barriers to group development. They state:

> The core of the theory of group development is that the principal obstacles to the development of valid communication are to be found in the orientations toward authority and intimacy that members bring to a group. Rebelliousness, submissiveness, or withdrawal as the characteristic response to authority figures; destructive competitiveness, emotional exploritiveness, or withdrawal as the characteristic response to peers present consensual validation of experience. The behaviors determined by these orientations are directed toward enslavement of the other in the service of the self, enslavement of the self in the service of the other, or disintegration of the situation. Hence, they prevent the setting, clarification of, and movement toward group-shared goals.[21]

We shall next consider the phase movements of the groups that encompass these problems of power and control.

PHASES IN GROUP DEVELOPMENT

Our fourth major area of concern is not a "problem" as we have used the term in the previous sections; rather group developmental phases are problems in the sense that each phase predictably presents problems to the participants in the group. Of several significant studies of the phases in a laboratory training group, we have selected two because of their apparent validity and generalizability to other groups.

Bennis and Shepard hypothesized two major phases in a group: *dependence* and *interdependence*.[22] Each in turn is divided into three subphases that we shall examine in some detail.

Subphase 1: dependence–flight.   Initially, time in a group is primarily concerned with problems of personal anxiety as the participants search out a common goal. Such security-seeking behaviors as sharing harmless facts about themselves and waiting for things to happen transpire in a highly ambiguous situation. Characteristically the group looks to the leader (trainer) to set up the rules and establish the system of rewards to fulfill the group's need for structure. When the trainer refrains from such action the ambiguity of the situation becomes intolerable and the trainer is perceived as the cause of the insecurity. Bennis and Shepard state:

During this phase the contributions made by members are designed to gain approval from the trainer, whose reaction to each comment is surreptitiously watched. If the trainer comments that this seems to be the case, or if he notes that the subject under discussion (say, discrimination) may be related to some concerns about membership in this group, he fails again to satisfy the needs of members. . . . The attempts to gain approval based on implicit hypotheses about the potential power of the trainer for good and evil are continued until the active members have been through the repertoire of behaviors that have gained them favor in the past.[23]

Subphase 2: counterdependence–flight. This subphase is likely the most stressful and unpleasant in the group's existence. As the trainer continues to fail to satisfy the group's needs, expressions of hostility (that were embarrassing in subphase 1) become more frequent and stronger. Power and leadership become topics of concern and two opposing subgroups are likely to emerge: one wishing to elect a chairperson, set up an agenda and structure the meetings; the other opposing all such efforts. Fragmentation is offered as an option and democratic techniques of voting are imposed. The absence of action by the trainer has created a "power gap" and no one is allowed to fill it. Simultaneously the group will likely attempt to punish the trainer for failures to meet the group's needs by ignoring his comments but secretly wishing that he will eventually lead them in the direction they should be going. "There is still the secret wish that the trainer will stop all the bedlam which has replaced polite uncertainty, by taking his proper role (so that the dependent members can cooperate with him and counterdependent can rebel in usual ways)."[24]

Subphase 3: resolution–catharsis. Up to this point the group is polarized into two competing subgroups, each unable to gain command. The trainer's comments now only deepen the wounds, and efforts at compromise by group members as yet uncommitted to the opposing camps are ineffective. The group is rapidly moving toward extinction. A sudden shift in the whole basis of the group's actions will probably occur. The independents (those uncommitted to either of the opposing groups) move into prime focus as the only potential source of the group's salvation. One of the group may now express the belief that the presense of the trainer is holding the group back and that the group would be better off without him. Bennis and Shepard cite the importance of this step:

> The principal function of the symbolic removal of the trainer is in its effect of freeing the group to bring into awareness the hitherto carefully ignored feeling toward him as an authority figure, and toward the group activity as an off-target dramatization of the ambivalence toward authority. ... The power problem is resolved by being defined in terms of member responsibilities, and the terms of the trainer's return to the group are settled by the requirement that he behave as "just another member of the group." This phrase is then explained as meaning that he should take neither more nor less responsibility for what happens in the group than any other member.[25]

Subphase 3 must be traversed before the group can move from dependence to interdependence. A group may be stuck for long periods of time in subphases 1 and 2, but the feelings are so intense in subphase 3 that a group passes through this level quickly. With the feeling that "we have now become a group" and "I am involved," the group moves into the three subphases of interdependence.

Subphase 4: enchantment–flight. At this point in time the group is cohesive, happy, and relaxed. A party mood predominates, and all decisions are made unanimously with major efforts made to "keep everyone happy." A new ambivalence emerges that is stated as follows: (1) "We all love one another and therefore we must maintain the solidarity of the group and give up whatever is necessary of our selfish desires"; and (2) "The group demands that I sacrifice my identity as a person; but the group is an evil mechanism which satisfies no dominant needs."[26] The mood of group belongingness thus meets with disenchantment as new anxieties emerge in the fake attempts to deny the existence of interpersonal problems.

Subphase 5: disenchantment–flight. Two subgroups again emerge as in subphase 2, but now based upon differences concerning the degree of intimacy required by group membership. One group is made up of "overpersonal" members demanding unconditional love, while a group of "counterpersonal" members resists any further involvement. A common theme underlies assumptions of both groups: "For the one group, the only means seen of maintaining self-esteem is to avoid any real commitment to others; for the other group, the only way to maintain self-esteem is to obtain a commitment from others to forgive everything. The subgroups share in common the fear that intimacy breeds contempt."[27] Thus in subphase 5 any further group involvement is viewed as potentially injurious to members' self-esteem.

Subphase 6: consensual validation.   As the time allotted for the group approaches termination (as with the end of a semester), pressures build that force the group toward resolution of the interdependency problem. If grades are involved, additional pressures are brought to bear. After arguments from the overpersonal who resist evaluation, and the pragmatic requirements of the course on the other, the independents typically request self-evaluations. A trust is expressed in the ability of group members to validate their self-concepts with other members. Bennis and Shepard note the following values that underlie the group's work in this subphase:

1. Members can accept one another's differences without associating "good" or "bad" with the differences.
2. Conflict exists but is over substantive issues rather than emotional issues.
3. Consensus is reached as a result of rational discussion rather than through a compulsive attempt at unanimity.
4. Members are aware of their own involvement, and of other aspects of group process, withoug being overwhelmed or alarmed.
5. Through the evaluation process, members take on greater personal meaning to each other. This facilitates communication and creates a deeper understanding of how the other person thinks, feels, behaves; it creates a series of personal expectations, as distinguished from the previous, more stereotyped role expectations.[28]

Thus, in the view of Bennis and Shepard, phases of dependence and interdependence are regarded as central problems of group life. These phases clearly reflect the relationship dimensions of dominance, affection, submission, and hostility that we discussed in chapter four. Typical patterns of group development can be predicted as groups move toward open, personal communication.

A second, similar description of the phases in a group's development has been made by Betty Meador.[29] She identified six stages in observing a group of eight people in an intensive weekend encounter lasting sixteen hours.

First stage.   The communication is about externals with no truly personal expressions. "Feelings and personal meanings are neither recognized nor owned. Constructs are extremely rigid. Close relationships are construed as dangerous."

Second stage. People are still communicating on "nonself" topics. "Feelings are sometimes described but as unowned past objects external to self. The individual is remote from his subjective experience." Contradictory expressions are not perceived as such, and any acknowledged problems or conflicts are dismissed as if they are external to the self.

Third stage. In this stage members describe feelings and personal meanings as past and distant, but not currently present. The self is discussed as an object or reflected object as perceived by others. There begins to emerge the recognition that "the problems that exist are inside the individual rather than external."

Fourth stage. There is now some expression of self-responsibility; problems, feelings, and personal meanings are for the first time owned by the self. Contradictions are recognized and explored. The people start to risk relating to one another on a feeling basis. "There is a dim recognition that feelings denied to awareness may break through in the present, but this is a frightening possibility. There is an unwilling, fearful recognition that one is *experiencing* things."

Fifth stage. Feelings are now communicated as they occur and are experienced at the present time with owned expressions, as we discussed in chapter two. The individual feels a growing responsibility for personal problems and questions the group on the validity of many constructs. "Feelings previously denied now tend to bubble through into awareness, though there is fear of this occurrence. There is some recognition that experiencing with immediacy is a referent and possible guide for the individual."

Sixth stage. Feelings that were previously denied are now experienced with immediacy that is dramatic, vivid, and cathartic to the individual and the group. The feelings are also accepted as a clear and useful referent in encountering the "real" self. The individuals risk disclosure by trusting the group. "The individual often feels somewhat 'shaky' as his solid constructs are recognized as construings that take place within him. The individual risks being himself in process in the relationship to others." As Meador states, "It is apparent that these individuals, initially strangers, attained a level of relating to each other not characteristic of ordinary life."

Each phase or stage in a group's development may be viewed as a barrier that must be crossed to open the way for further involvement in the relationships. Each phase or stage is necessary, critical, and crucial at the time of its emergence. The group's progress may be measured by the ease and/or rapidity (and avoidance of repetition) with which each of these crucial barriers is overcome.

SUMMARY

We have discussed four areas of common problems that plague most laboratory groups: *Distrust and defensiveness* are characteristic of the early stages of a group's life and impede open, personal communication from occurring. Similarly, a *lack of cohesion and group compatability* has been shown to be directly related to the investment that the individual makes in the group, the acceptance of the group's goals by each individual, and satisfaction within the group. Questions of *power and control* must be handled in order not to be manipulative of individuality, preserving the options of choice by each member of the group. Coercion and manipulation are antithetical to the growth that is desired by each member of the group. Finally, we have noted that each of the *phases in group development* is a critical problem at the time of its occurrence and progression stages of group process and barriers are highly probable and predictable.

Throughout this chapter we have encountered the dilemma of personal independence versus the need to interact with others. On the one hand, people need people and we *need* to interact with others. On the other, we also *need* to maintain our individual identity. We can never completely satisfy the one without suffering some loss of the other. There is no easy final answer for this dilemma: we constantly shift our emphasis and search for new ways of satisfying both needs.

If a relationship is to be established and endure, there are foreseeable problems that must be met and overcome. Only when we trust other people, feel that we are accepted by the group and can accept the group's goals, work out to mutual satisfaction issues of power and control, and progress through predictable stages of growth, can we be expected to engage in meaningful, personal communication and reap the benefits of personal growth in the laboratory group.

6

hElpiNq pEoplE
To iMpROVE ThEiR RElATioNShips
wiTh oThERS

Implicit in our earlier chapters is the major significance of the laboratory training group leader to the total process of developing personal
communication and group growth. It is our belief that a laboratory
training group leader is not a person with a special set of social skills,
a little bag of tricks, or familiarity with a flock of exercises. Rather,
he is a person who has reliable information and insight regarding
human interaction, and uses this knowledge to help group members
find more satisfying ways of relating to each other.

Just as the groups themselves have an assortment of labels, all the
currently used labels for the laboratory group leader seem to us
misleading and inappropriate. To refer to this person as "instructor,"
"teacher," or "leader" immediately projects an authoritarian role
expectation. "Trainer" similarly conjures up the figure of a manipulative individual forcing people to jump through hoops and the like.
"Facilitator" places a special burden on this individual and seems to
imply that the other members of the group are not likewise facilitative individuals. Rather than become enmeshed in a semantic exercise, however, we shall use these terms as synonymous labels for the
person designated as "leader."

In this chapter we shall note the differences in "trainer styles," examine research on the role of the trainer, cite special problems of the trainer in academic groups, and cite ways that the trainer can help people achieve growth-producing encounters.

TRAINER STYLES

In an early study (1955) of trainer roles in laboratory training, Bennis and Schein developed several assumptions.[1] One was that the issue of trainer characteristics is one of the most important and also one of the most difficult to unscramble in terms of what we actually know versus what our own biases and prejudices lead us to believe. The most obvious generalization is that the trainer's theories, personality, background, and experiences will influence the goals and training design of the laboratory. Personality refers to those personal characteristics which set limits on the kinds of situations he can handle.

Differences Between Laboratory Group Leaders and Therapy Group Leaders

In chapter one we cited basic theoretical differences between the educational laboratory group and the therapy group. Our question now is: What are the differences in the roles and functions of a T-group leader and a therapy group leader? Both groups have common features such as both are learning situations to bring about change; both stress learning to communicate accurately; and both value mature, group-centered, and responsible functioning of members—therapy groups because it is a sign of improvement of individual patients and T-groups because it improves group functioning. Therefore, back to our original question, where and how do the leaders differ?

First, according to Frank, in therapy groups there is an irreducible gap between the leader and the members, because the leader is in the role of a practitioner of a healing art from which the patients hope to benefit.[2] The trainer of a T-group differs from the members only in the possession of superior knowledge and skill in certain areas. To the extent that he successfully imparts this knowledge, the gap between him and the group members progressively diminishes until, at the end of a successful T-group experience, there is little difference between trainer and other members of the group.

In general, the therapy group more actively protects its members and is also more threatening to them. In therapy groups there is no limit to the task, which is personal modification in its broadest sense. In T-groups, the task is limited to the elucidation of group-relevant attitudes. In therapy groups, the process is reversed; overt behavior is used as a means of elucidating underlying motivations. Depending on the therapist's theory of psychotherapy, this may involve more or less extensive investigation of historical roots of the patient's current feelings. Thus, the trainer of a T-group reviews different attitudes toward the trainer, but refrains from identifying the members involved. In treatment groups, this identification would occur as a matter of course. This adds to the threat of the situation.

Just as T-groups try not to stir up too much anxiety, so, usually, do they make less effort to offer explicit support. They do not hesitate at times to expose the distorted perceptions of a member, on the assumption that he can tolerate this without undue anxiety and can learn from the experience. In therapy groups, this exposure is frequently made also; but the therapist always has in mind how much the patient can stand and is prepared to intervene, if necessary.

The National Training Laboratory (NTL) Trainer Model

The NTL had its beginning in the summer of 1947 when a workshop in group development was held at Gould Academy in Bethel, Maine. Joint sponsors were the National Education Association and the Research Center for Group Dynamics of the Massachusetts Institute of Technology. The basic research was supported by a grant from the Office of Naval Research. One of the features of this workshop was a small continuing group, called the Basic Skills Training Group, in which an anecdotal observer made observational data available for discussion and analysis by the group. The training leader helped the group to analyze and evaluate these data, supplemented with data from the participants and from the training leader.[3] This BST Group was designed as a medium for several kinds of learnings. It had, as one of its main functions, the development of a clearer understanding of democratic values. Those values were to operate in terms of principles of methodology for functioning as a trainer or member of a group and as an initiator and facilitator of change.

The general objectives agreed upon by the workshop faculty, in terms of the trainer's role, were: (1) work with group members in developing plans that are agreeable to all of them instead of telling them what they are to do and how they are to do it; (2) make statements which are intended to guide rather than direct; (3) be responsible for making a frequent oral inventory of progress and for stating whether or not the group is staying on the path that will take them to their goal; (4) work with all group members on the task of evaluating how effectively they are working together; the trainer should see it as his authority to stop the discussion long enough for the members to look at themselves as a working group; (5) give expert information only when it is pertinent to the situation and only when it is appropriate; and (6) support the development of spontaneous shifts in the group's activity which are in line with the policy agreed upon by them.[4]

The workshop members believed that leadership behavior is a complex function of many interdependent variables. Leadership behavior occurs in a variety of situations and is determined in no small measure by the nature of the particular environment in which the leader perceives himself functioning, as well as by the characteristics of the person who is doing the leading. These objectives demand unassertiveness, social sensitivity, and supportive behavior.[5]

In the "normal T-group training models," the importance of the group trainer is basically self-explanatory. The potential for personal growth and reduction of the risk of personal damage in the group experience requires trainers with a high professional competence, a dedication of purpose, a genuine interest in the well-being of people, an openness toward others and toward new experiences, experience in group process, and a trust in that process.

Blake and Mouton, from their work with instrumental groups (using self-administered rating scales, rankings, etc.), have stated that the primary role of the trainer is to aid feedback by calling attention to critical events occurring within the group.[6] He creates the conditions and provides the model for members to become participant-observers of group action. The trainer also helps the group to explore ground rules appropriate for personal evaluation. In other words, in a trainer-directed group, one important focus on trainer-intervention is on establishing the feedback model.

Blake and Mouton identify three specific questions which they feel the trainer must consider: (1) When should I (the trainer) intervene? They suggest that trainer interventions should decrease as member participant-observer contributions increase. If he is successful in introducing the participant-observer role, his interventions are less frequent in later rather than in earlier group meetings. (2) At what level or "depth" should I (the trainer) make remarks about some critical process event? One procedure is for me to intervene in order to focus attention on events for which the motivations and assump-

tions are likely to be evident. The direction, therefore, is from sur-
face to depth. The direction is dictated by the fact that as insights
develop into the dynamics of group functioning they can be used to
produce more fundamental insights. This level or depth of interventions is likely to become the standard for participant-observer evaluation by members. Thus, it is important that the trainer lead rather
than follow members in the pursuit of more fundamental explorations. (3) How can I establish the participant-observer orientation,
while avoiding becoming an "expert" and creating more dependency reactions? The participant-observer orientation should not be
introduced by "stunning" the group with brilliant interpretations. In
any event, Blake and Mouton's rationale is that members learn about
group functioning primarily by developing their own insights. They
learn only incidentally by accepting the trainer's account of some
process event. Members' adoption of this rationale can go far toward
solving the dependency problems.

Divergent Approaches to the Problem of Trainer and Role

Gordon notes that there exist two fundamentally different philosophical positions about the nature of people which lead to different
pathways we might travel in the search for patterns of trainer roles.[7]
If a negative and disparaging view of people predominates, the general approach to the problem of a trainer's role will be an attempt
to discover new and better ways of enhancing the control of the
trainer over their group. But, if a more positive and hopeful philosophy prevails, then we would predict that the general approach is an
attempt to discover new and better ways of developing the potentials
of groups, of freeing individuals to assume more responsibility and
control over their destinies.

The leader-centered approach.   Those who, by nature, view people
as being in need of strong leadership, are in accord with this approach. This disparaging view of humanity means that the trainer
should attempt to discover and perfect methods by which he can
more accurately diagnose and assess the needs, opinions, and attitudes of those whom he is to lead. Possessing accurate information
of this kind, the trainer should be in a much better position to decide
what is best for his group.

Trainers who follow the leader-guided approach advocate that the
most effective group is one in which each member can contribute his
maximum potential. Member's spontaneous and creative behavior

will in the long run be of most help to the group. Mature groups have the capacity for making sound decisions and reaching effective solutions to their problems. Groups can best learn to utilize the potential of each member by depending at first on the guidance of their leader. New groups may not have the skills and capacities for self-determined, self-responsible behavior, so it must be taught them by the trainer. Goals set by the trainer will be beneficial, although eventually a group should be mature enough to set its own goals.

Change can be facilitated by bringing to bear the influence of the trainer's ideas, insights, and knowledge. Group leadership should be vested in a trainer who has experience, knowledge, maturity, skills, insights, and so on. A group situation should always be structured in such a way that it contains "a trainer." Groups demand structure; without it they will be anxious.

The trainer of a leader-centered approach finds out as much as possible about the group's needs, in order to provide the group with a situation where it can get what it needs. He plans specific learning situations and/or group experiences from which the group may draw insights. Preparation involves doing things that will improve his own contribution and things that he feels the group needs. By using his influence or his special status position in the group, he is able to guide it in certain directions. He wants the group members to use him as a resource person.

The trainer often influences or directly manipulates members to play some particular role. He usually accedes to members' wishes that he play some particular role or else tries to convince them that another role is best. He often interprets the group's behavior in order to give members understandings they might not acquire themselves. He tries to be perceived as "the trainer" believing that he will thus be better able to control the situation to meet the group's needs.

The group-centered approach. The group-centered approach has as its basic philosophy that it is the responsibility of the trainer to discover ways by which each individual group member may learn to clarify and diagnose his own needs and learn how to achieve self-understanding. The trainer should make an effort to create the necessary conditions to free the individual from overdependence on the skills and insights of the "expert."

This approach involves focusing on questions essentially concerned with enhancing the group rather than its leader. It calls for the trainer to address himself to questions that are distinctively different from those that become the focus when the subject is approached from a trainer-centered view. The group-centered approach is concerned with discovering methods of developing the potentialities of group members so that they may become more capable of constructive self-direction—in fact, so that they may become less dependent upon their trainer and free to take an active part in shaping their own destinies.

Further philosophical views include the fact that the most effective group is one in which each member can contribute his maximum potential. Groups have the capacity for making sound decisions and reaching effective solutions to their problems. A group can best learn to utilize the potential of each member when it is free from dependence on a formal trainer or some other authority. Goals set by the group will be most beneficial to it. Change that is significant and enduring must be self-initiated. Self-initiated change will take place most effectively in a nonthreatening, accepting psychological atmosphere.

The trainer using the group-centered approach allows the group to diagnose its own needs. He tries to facilitate this process by allowing the group to plan its own experiences. By avoiding making decisions for the group (except those which facilitate bringing members together initially) he improves his contribution.

If at all possible, the trainer will try to lose his "special status" position so that he can participate in decision making without having his contributions given special attention or consideration. He wants to contribute resources just like any other member of the group, rather than as a special resource person. The trainer must put himself on the same level with the other members. He should try not to think beyond the level of expressed understanding of group members, feeling that only meaningful insights will be those arrived at by members themselves. He tries not to be perceived as "the leader," believing that as long as he is so perceived, members will not be completely free to be themselves and often will react to his contributions either submissively and uncritically or with hostility and resistance. By trying to lose the "official role" he is free to resist the group's needs for dependence and to reduce his own anxiety about the outcome of group action.

Our philosophical preference is definitely on the side of the group-centered style of leadership. The stated assumptions of the earlier chapter testify to this fact. The phase developments in a group discussed in chapter five are based on the implicit assumptions of a group-centered leader. Thus, we are on the side of Carl Rogers in his debate with B. F. Skinner discussed in the previous chapter. We believe that available research on group growth in the laboratory setting validates our position. Let us now examine such research.

RESEARCH ON THE ROLE OF THE TRAINER

Several recent studies have been concerned with the trainer's impact and effects of different styles of training. In one study Culbert varied the amount of "self-disclosing" done by a trainer working with two training groups. He discovered that while both groups eventually reached the same level of increased self-awareness, the group with the more self-disclosing leader did so earlier. He suggested that openness on the part of the trainer served as a model for the other members of the group.[8]

Lomranz surveyed the goals and intervention patterns of over one hundred experienced trainers. By factor analysis, he isolated three distinct categories of stated goals: (1) "personal and interpersonal learning," the goal to which the current authors ascribe as just and foremost; (2) "personal and interpersonal expanded experiencing," referring obviously to expanding levels of awareness and consciousness; and (3) "personal and interpersonal corrective experiencing," designating self-improvement and therapeutic goals as foremost. While no clearcut patterns of interventions were common to any one group, it was discovered that the trainers selecting the second goal were younger, less experienced, more authoritarian, and less interested in group processes than the trainers placing emphasis on the first and third goals.[9]

Perhaps the most revealing and pertinent of the studies was made by Irvin Yalom and Morton Lieberman and focused attention upon the "casualties" of the laboratory group experience.[10] Eighteen encounter groups made up of 209 undergraduate students met for a total of thirty hours. Of the 209 students, sixteen were classified as "casualties," defined as "an enduring, significant, negative outcome which was caused by their participation in the group."[11]

According to Yalom and Lieberman:

A major finding of the study is that the number and severity of casualties and the manner in which the casualties sustained injury are all highly dependent upon the particular type of encounter group. Some leadership styles result in a high-risk group.

Particularly stressful is a leader style (type A) which is characterized by intensive, aggressive stimulation, by high charisma, by high challenging and confrontation of each of the members, and by authoritarian control.[12]

These type A leaders were forceful, impatient, and demanded change in their group members *"now."* Further, they made little differentiation in the various needs of individuals in their groups assuming that everyone should accomplish the same thing.

By contrast, there was low-risk in groups led by type B leaders. "The type B leaders offered considerable positive support for members. They helped create an accepting, trusting climate in the group which permitted members to participate at their own pace."[13]

The educational laboratory training experience should not be undertaken by someone in need of therapy; it is no substitute for psychiatric counseling or group work. However, for the "average" person, the experience entails no special threat in the hands of a type B leader. Indeed, Yalom and Lieberman note that while their research was primarily concerned with the potential hazards of the group experience, "we wish to remind the reader that the positive gains from the experience were far-reaching for many subjects."[14] Thus, it appears to us that there is reasonable data to support our claim for a group-centered style of leadership.

SPECIAL PROBLEMS WITH ACADEMIC GROUPS

There appear to be two essential differences in trainer role behavior in the academic setting.

First, the trainer working with academic groups cannot easily divorce himself from certain aspects of the legitimized authority of the normal teacher role. A grading system must be administered and grades must be turned in. This is the case even when we set up a contract so that a large part of the grading is devised and administered by the group as a whole. In addition, the academic trainer must be concerned with such matters as attendance.

There is the strong temptation for the academic trainer to regard himself as the "teacher" and remain in a traditional, "protected" academic role. This is complemented by the role perceptions of group members (students) who see the trainer only through the distorted lens of their feelings about a generalized authority figure directly comparable to other instructors in the university. This situation is not found in the usual laboratory setting where trainers might be identified as "staff" but then have little or no institutional power at their command such as the ability to reward and punish.

The topic of the correspondence between socially acquired modes of relating to authority and the potency of the trainer's role in the

T-group was partially covered when discussing the concept of phases in group development in chapter five. Even when the trainer's role is conceived of as that of a neutral resource person, it is likely that belief in this concept is limited to the trainer alone. It seems that the effect he has on the group is tied in with the influence and authority he holds in the member's minds. The manifold duties ascribed to the trainer (such as serving as a role model, interpreting, emphasizing feelings and emotions, being permissive) are effective because the authoritative nature of his role remains prominent, and is not "worked through." The educational trainer does not become a *non*-authority; he becomes a different kind of authority. This is not to suggest that members' learning and relationships to authority figures does not change, but rather that the changes are quantitative rather than qualitative. The possibilities for understanding authority figures become widened. This group conception of the academic trainer is related to the societal expectations of him, i.e. he continues to remain the symbol of the ultimate external referent, and by taking advantage of this, is able to show by positive sanctioning that there are other types of permissible behavior.

The implications of this situation for trainer interventions are important. The academic trainer has at least two alternatives open to him. First, there is the temptation to alter the academic situation to make it as comparable as possible to the typical laboratory setting. The trainer can minimize his legitimate authority by putting grading and course administration almost completely into the hands of the group. One extreme possibility along these lines would be to offer no academic credit for human relations training courses. In addition, the trainer can so structure the course, using devices such as separate theory sessions, so that his behavior in the training group can more closely conform to the expectations of other group members.

The other alternative is more satisfying to us. The trainer can recognize the complexity of his reality situation and capitalize on it by his participation. Instead of presenting a relatively bland screen to group members he can help them to analyze and understand their varying reactions to an authority figure who presents, in actuality, many different faces and behaviors to the group. In doing this, subjects' expectations of and past relationships with authority figures can be studied, along with their present reactions to an authority figure-member-observer-resource person who is not and cannot be all one piece. In the final analysis, this situation is not dissimilar to the actual situation which students will encounter in organizational or family roles.

The second, related problem is that the academic trainer, to a much greater extent than the trainer in human relations laboratories, is responsible for cognitive structuring of the training experience, both to provide some cognitive support for the emotional experience of group members, and to satisfy needs for specific kinds of information or experience. (These may be his needs and/or those of group members.) Thus, the academic trainer may lecture, provide reading assignments, lead his group in skill practice exercises, etc. This cognitive structuring must often be provided during the context of the training group meeting.

To the extent that laboratory trainers participate in theory session presentations, and lead their groups in skill practice sessions, their role differentiation becomes increasingly complex, and the differences between academic trainers and laboratory trainers are minimized. We believe that practice and behaviors in the group can and should be tied to a body of theoretical data. The goal of this book is to provide such data.

In summary, it appears that perceptions of the academic trainer, and reactions to him, are conditioned by (1) the legitimatized framework of power and authority within which he operates; and (2) the greater role flexibility in the conception of "trainer" that is demanded of him by the situation. Both of these are less noticeable in the reaction to trainers in a laboratory setting. On the other hand, because of the lack of role structuring for the laboratory trainer, and the greater possibility for behavioral ambiguity which this affords, perceptions of the trainer can be seen more in terms of the discrepancy between his actual ambiguous performance and the expectations and past reactive dispositions which group members bring to the situation.

GUIDELINES FOR THE TRAINER

How can a person who is experienced in developing good human relations help others to achieve growth-producing encounters? We would suggest eight behaviors for the trainer or any facilitative person in a group.

1. Model productive interaction. An effective way of helping others to learn is to provide a good example. Laboratory learning includes both participating and observing. You can help others by letting them see that you believe in the process, by doing nothing to diminish the trust others are placing in you, and by demonstrating the behaviors suggested in the following guidelines.

2. Focus on the present—"the here and now."   As we noted in chapters two and three, it is helpful to talk mostly about the present, that which is mainly under the control of those persons who are currently interacting. Such "here and now" data is fresh and of primary interest, and all who are present can learn by facilitating tentative, exploratory changes in the interpersonal relationships. Actually, the "here and now focus" can include that recent past which has been *experienced together* by the members of a dyad or group; focusing on *shared experience* is of more value than trying to stick very close to the precise present.

3. Encourage the quest for personal feedback.   The human relations learning paradigm is as follows:

  a. Few people are completely satisfied with themselves (i.e. their view of themselves or their self-image).
  b. Most people are interested in seeing how others, especially new acquaintances, respond to them.
  c. If there seems to be a discrepancy between their self-image and the way they appear to be seen by or to affect others, a motive for possible change (learning) has been generated.
  d. A mature person will recognize that he does not *have to change* just because of this discrepancy; it is his alternative or choice.
  e. Change followed by favorable feedback produces a strong learning (change) situation.

Feedback becomes of prime importance. It can be helpful if a stable, unthreatened person encourages (but does not demand) feedback from others. This feedback consists of others telling you how they perceive you and how they feel about you.

4. Preserve individual choice regarding change.   Even though feedback has been requested or subtly sought by a person and consequently received, his *right to choose to change or not to change* should be preserved. We know that simple behavioral changes can be induced by operant conditioning, but unless such changes are desired by the "subject," the effort can backfire, and negative attitudes plus firm resolution to "never change" can be the result. It can be helpful to others if you make certain they understand your willingness (only if sincere) to let them make the choice themselves.

Many of the alleged malpractices in T-groups can be avoided if *opportunity to choose to change or not change* is preserved.

5. Support attempts of others to change their behavior. Once a person makes known that he has decided to try to behave differently, the early efforts at change need your support. Encouragement will be needed to attempt desired changes, and *tension* induced by attempts to change may cause the person to behave in a less desirable way at first. Tolerance of tense behavior is helpful. Some persons will quietly resolve to change without communicating their commitment; you should be alert to minor changes and encourage (reward or compliment) them in an unobtrusive (unembarrassing) way.

6. Develop helpful interaction norms. From psychotherapy and counseling studies, three ways of interacting have been identified as helpful:

   a. *Show accurate empathy* with the way the other person feels; showing that you know *how* he feels, not just *why* he feels that way.
   b. Extend *nonpossessive warmth,* i.e. regard for the other person as a *person* with real potential *without* predicating the continuation of such warmth on behavior or change desired by you. This kind of warmth has no restrictions or "strings" tied to it. (This way of interacting is not easy to achieve unless sincerely felt; it is identifiable when you and the other person have together "joined hands to face the common enemy"— his problem, anxiety, or desire to behave differently.)
   c. Behave in a way that is *congruent* with your feelings. Sometimes this is called "being genuine," i.e. being true to your innermost feelings, expressing your anger or anxiety when honestly felt, but still expressing it in a way that does not deny the other person nonpossessive warmth nor accurate empathy.

Few people can actually behave in all three ways at the same time, but you should try to do some of each whenever you can. If you can help to establish these three ways of behaving as norms for your dyad or group, members can grow and help you (and others) to grow into more satisfying ways of relating to others.

7. Allow individual defensive behavior. While it is desirable to diminish artificial barriers between people, it is also very important *not* to tear them down too fast. Individuals who insist on maintaining themselves through defensive behavior should be allowed to do so without pressure or diatribe—*so long as they have been told how they are perceived* by others. *The choice of changing their behavior should remain theirs.*

8. Preserve human dignity.   At no time in trying to relate to others does a person need to abandon basic human dignity. You can empathize and show nonpossessive warmth toward a person who is ill, dirty, ignorant, perverted, and/or vicious without *becoming* sick, dirty, stupid, gross, or mean. In fact, behaving like a person who is in trouble when you are with a troubled person may not be helpful to that person at all. Genuine *consideration* of the motives, habits, perceptions, and feelings of others is the keynote to interpersonal harmony.

Artifacts of human dignity (for example, status symbols such as neckties and ceremonial robes which tend to separate people) may need to be laid aside. Artificial forms of separation, if clung to by one or more persons, will likely keep them psychologically apart. But it is very important to determine behaviors and accouterments which tend to separate people and those which do not. Barriers *designed* to keep people apart, such as wide conference tables, should be avoided, while different colored socks (or no socks) will make no difference *if it is not taken to mean a difference,* i.e. a social distinction or barrier. While it is true that elimination of artificial social barriers is necessary to improve interpersonal human relations, hundreds of laboratory groups have demonstrated that people can make satisfactory progress without frolicking nude, smelling each other's armpits, or crudely degrading sexual enjoyment—that is, without joining the oft-cited lunatic fringe of sensitivity training.

SUMMARY

In this chapter we have noticed the different approaches to group leadership that are possible. Our preference is for the group-centered approach in which the trainer assumes a nonauthoritarian role as an open, facilitative member of the group who refuses to make its decisions. Research cited shows this leadership style to be less threatening and potentially less damaging even to people who should not be in the laboratory group.

We have noted the special problems of the instructor/teacher in training a laboratory group in an academic environment and have suggested that an honest exploration of the limits of legitimate power can be a meaningful learning experience for everyone concerned.

Finally we have suggested that the trainer/facilitative person can make great contributions by modeling productive interaction, by focusing on the present, by encouraging personal feedback, by helping preserve individual choice regarding change and supporting attempts of others for change, by developing interaction norms of empathy, nonpossessive warmth, and congruency, allowing defensive behaviors where needed, and preserving human dignity. These ideals of human conduct will be difficult to achieve totally, but to the extent that we are successful, we will help people to improve their relationship with others.

7

CONfRONTATiON iN
HUMAN RELATiONS
TRAiNiNG

We live our lives in terms of our images of ourselves; our self-images tend to govern our behavior. In like manner we tend to interact with others in ways determined by our self-images. We initiate interactions in ways that fit our notions of how we can and should (or should not) reach out to contact others. Our images of our world and ourselves in it heavily influence our interpersonal relationships.[1]

To the extent that our images of ourselves are pleasing or satisfactory, our behavior tends to be stable, repetitive, and unchanging. When we receive information that disturbs our satisfactory image of ourselves, behavioral change becomes a real possibility. In many cases when a person is confronted with data that causes him to reconsider his self-image, that is, when data is received that contradicts an existing self-perception, he will turn to new modes of behavior that are likely to produce a more desirable self-concept. Confrontation with a new perception of oneself, a change in self-awareness, is the subject of this chapter.

A new and unsatisfactory self-perception can be a disturbing experience. *Nothing in life, for most of us, is more important than our feelings about ourselves.* An undesirable self-awareness can produce considerable strain or stress. On the other hand, such an experience can be a valuable contribution to personal growth and improved interpersonal behavior. It can also point the way, indicate the type of change needed or the direction in which a person needs to go if he wishes to be more effective in his interpersonal relations. Thus, the most valuable and the most distressing type of interaction can occur all in the same interpersonal event. That is why the behavior described in the present chapter is so important.

When two people are together, nothing *never* happens. You cannot be in the presence of someone and present *no* messages concerning your relationship. Failure to respond to your presence (regardless if it is unintentional) becomes a comment on the relationship. Silence in your presence tells you how you are perceived by the other person. When two people are together and one attempts to initiate interaction, he may simply be requesting information or an opinion about some unimportant item, such as, "Is anyone intending to sit there?" In every such case, implicit in such behavior is an important but subtle request: "Please validate me." The implicit, underlying question is: "Will you please respond to me as a person—a worthwhile human being entitled to common courtesy and consideration?"[2]

Even though an attempt to initiate interaction may appear to be a simple request for recognition of one's ideas ("What do you think of my suggestion for our vacation?"), inherent in every such event is a clear implication regarding the value of oneself personally. In any interpersonal situation it is impossible to refuse to respond to the implicit request: "Please validate me." An attempt to *avoid* giving a response denies the existence of the other person on a functional, interpersonal, or communicational level.[3]

The question of validity is implied in every statement we make to another person. Whenever we talk we implicitly ask this same question. In this way we are constantly requesting information that relates to our self-image. At almost any time we may receive information that can disturb our satisfaction with our view of ourselves. When such data are received it is obvious that we should check them out very carefully. Did the other person *intend* this message? Is a *misunderstanding* involved?

It has been our observation that the implicit request, "Please validate me," and attendant responses, have not been given careful consideration by most of us. In this chapter we will look very carefully at ways in which these messages occur and the ways in which we can treat them. Confrontation by such information is very serious psychological business; how we use or misuse messages can make an important difference to our personal growth and our satisfaction with our lives.

THE DYNAMICS OF CONFRONTATION

We try to change our environment whenever we are confronted by seriously undesirable elements. In like manner we tend to change our behavior when we are confronted by an undesirable self-image. The essence of confrontation as we are using the term here is that, in one way or another, a person *sees himself in a way that is new or different*. In laboratory training groups this new awareness is often brought about by a "reflection" of ourselves from others—feedback indicating their view of us. In this way confrontation may occur between a person and those others from whom he receives feedback.

A classic use of the term *confrontation* is to refer to social conflict and consequent clash between disagreeing parties; this disagreement is usually over some important social issue. Disagreement and social conflict is not what we are concerned about in this chapter. In our use of the term we are concerned with conflict within a person about his view of himself—new self-insight or self-awareness that is in disagreement with important parts of his previous self-image. The fact that this new self-awareness is often brought about by feedback from others is important. However, the essential element is that a person eventually confronts himself with this new information. In this section we are concerned with the way in which this occurs.

We Obtain New Information About Ourselves

The basic element in self-confrontation is the acquisition of new information about ourselves. As a matter of fact, new information is almost constantly available. New circumstances for interaction routinely arise. Even if the persons with whom we interact are well-known associates, these new circumstances provide opportunities to see how they respond to us. For example, one of your friends may be offered a new job, or be absent from work for a week with the flu, or have a baby, or get a ticket for speeding. How we respond to their circumstances provides opportunity for them to receive feedback on how we see them—if they are really interested in the information.

Many times we tend to avoid or ignore opportunities for feedback. We insulate ourselves from new and valuable information about ourselves. Human relations training groups are deliberately designed to provide this information by encouraging us to look at ourselves, to consider the responses of others, and to listen to feedback about the way we are perceived.[4] These training groups try to promote new insights and self-awareness. In a human relations training group led by one of the present authors, one member of the group soon emerged as leader. He clarified and restated group issues. Responses to comments by others were directed toward him, often using certain words he had used. Group decisions or viewpoints were summarized by him. Apparently, he was not aware of the extent to which he was engaged in such behavior. Eventually, one of the other members said, "All my life I have wanted to be a leader. When I work with a group, I try to get them to listen to me. How come when I say something to this group no one seems to respond to me? But when he *restates* what I say, you respond to him as if it were his own idea?" The discussion which followed provided considerable feedback on the behavior of both individuals.

An encounter group for human relations training in which a person is never confronted by new perceptions of himself is a weak group, of questionable value in terms of learning to improve one's capabilities in interpersonal relations. It is assumed that an individual enters a group because he wants to examine his way of relating to others. It is reasonable to expect that he will receive new information that may provide stimulation for growth and change. This new information always carries an implicit invitation to reflect upon one's behavior and to consider possible changes.[5]

We Reconsider Our Self-Image

If new information *supports* our image of ourselves we tend to continue our usual behavior. If it enhances our image, makes it more appealing to us, we tend to increase that image-enhancing behavior. If, on the other hand, our new information lowers our self-estimation, we usually give some consideration to the possibility of changing our behavior.[6] After the discussion of the incident in the group described above, the member who had emerged as a leader said he believed he should try to respond to the ideas of others as *their own* ideas and not just funnel the group interaction through himself. The other member said he would try to see that he "did just that!"

Ordinarily only a small part of our self-image is involved with any new information. Sometimes we can ignore data; at other times we can provide adequate consideration without feeling that much of our selfhood is involved. If vital parts or most of our self-image is involved, serious anxiety may be aroused. If our image is seriously diminished or damaged, desperate and deep depression may result. In extreme cases, serious mental disturbance, even suicide, occurs.[7]

We Scan the Behavioral Horizon

As we consider changing our behavior, we consider our options. Can we change in ways that might be beneficial? Have we tried before? Do we know others who behave this way? Were they always thus or did they successfully undergo some change? Are such changes foreign to our usual behavioral habits? Are they actually within our physical and emotional capability? For example, if we have a violent temper and occasionally attack one of our associates with great verbal severity, is it possible for us to interact with less violence? Can we really learn to hold our temper? Can we learn to show our displeasure quickly and easily before it gets out of hand?

We also consider the possible costs and potential rewards of changes that appear to be desirable and available to us.[8] For example, will people think we are irritating if we go around disagreeing with them over little things? On the other hand, will our own emotional wear and tear be diminished if we do that instead of suffering our usual blow-ups? Will others respond to us more satisfactorily if we disagree more frequently and blow up less?

In the final analysis only the individual involved can determine what a possible change will produce for him in terms of personal costs and rewards; he will apply a personal set of values for emotional expenses and interaction assets. If a decision to change is to be of long-range satisfaction, it must be made by the individual involved. Other people can give him feedback; they can tell him how he is perceived and how they feel about the perception. But only he can arrive at a decision that will be of lasting value to himself.

We Try New Behavior

Like a new pair of shoes, newly acquired interpersonal behavior feels stiff and awkward. At first we tend to "try it on for size," see how it fits us, how it feels. We are self-conscious and uneasy. As we note how we feel while behaving in our new way, we also note how others seem to be responding to us.[9]

Like learning to fly a light airplane, we approach our new behavior with some anticipation and anxiety. If we are successful in our attempt to fly—if we make a satisfactory landing—we feel exhilarated and very pleased. Likewise if our new interpersonal behavior brings rewarding responses from others, we feel gratified. In so doing, we gain a new self-image, a new awareness of ourselves as persons who can change in desirable directions. We achieve a new perspective on our potential, new insights into our possibilities for changing, and new hope for more successful ways of interacting with others.

Such an expanded vision of oneself and one's potential can be extremely valuable.[10] A new self-image can be fully as exciting and rewarding as learning to fly an airplane. In many cases it can be very valuable in terms of enhancing one's joy in living a deeper and more satisfying life.

We Stabilize Our New Successful Behaviors

If succeeding experiments with our new behaviors continue to produce rewarding responses, we tend to make these ways routine and habitual. We grow more comfortable as the new behaviors become established. We use them on more occasions and work out new variations and modifications. Eventually they become assimilated into a new self-image, and we think of ourselves as "that kind of person," one who behaves in these ways in certain situations. Our anxiety diminishes and our self-image is enhanced.[11]

Not all new, experimental behaviors are successful. Sometimes we incur trouble. Sometimes, like the student-pilot who has a poor landing, we receive a jolt. At times we may fail to achieve our hopes or aspirations, and feel we just cannot do what we see others doing. Sometimes this may be true. More frequently, however, we have observed members of encounter groups try to experiment with new behaviors, suffer setbacks and discouragement, try again, and achieve results that were personally very satisfying.

In attempting to improve one's ways of relating to other people, setbacks should be anticipated, periods of discouragement should be expected, and more than a single series of attempts should be made.[12] As we have suggested earlier (in chapter three), changing one's interpersonal behavior is not easy; it will ordinarily require continued and determined effort.

The dynamic process of obtaining new personal information, redefining oneself, changing one's interpersonal behavior, and deriving a new self-image are all serious psychological processes.[13] They deal with what, to most of us, is the most important thing in the world —our personal feelings about *ourselves*.

SOURCES OF CONFRONTIVE DATA

At this point we are directing attention to the ways in which we can obtain new data about ourselves. Of course, we are primarily interested in data that relate to our interpersonal behavior—ways in which we relate, well or not so well, to other people. There are three primary sources of such data: our own observations, feedback from others, and overt requests for us to change.[14]

Our Own Perceptions

If we really wish to take a careful look at ourselves we can learn a great deal from observing our responses to other people.[15] For example, as we meet a group of strangers or persons we know only slightly, do we initiate interaction? Do we take the lead? Do we find ourselves to be outgoing or inhibited? When others attempt to initiate a conversation with us, do we respond easily and in a friendly way?

If we interact well with one other person, how do we behave in a group? Do we tend to hide in the group, withdraw from the interaction, avoid raising questions and interact uneasily with respondents? How do we handle another's show of regard or affection toward us? Do we behave in a way that shows appreciation, makes the other person feel at ease, perhaps willing to show us warmth and friendship again?

How do we *feel* as we interact with others? Our perceptions of our feelings are very valuable, although somewhat subject to restrictions or distortions, as are all perceptions. They are particularly valuable because only we are actually able to perceive *directly* our feelings. Other people must gain information about our feelings by what we tell them or by indirect inferences based upon their perceptions of our behavior.[16] As we interact with others, to what extent are we comfortable? Anxious? Do we feel defensive about letting others know very much about us? Is our hostility easily aroused? Do we spend a large share of our time in a group feeling angry? Frustrated?

Our own perception of the ways in which others respond to us can give us good clues to important information about our interpersonal behavior. We must remember that these observations only provide clues to how we are being seen by them—clues in the sense that, from such, we can only indirectly infer that they see us as dominant or submissive, friendly or hostile. Some behaviors in our presence are not really responses to us. An interesting part of our behavior may have gone unnoticed by the other person.[17] Very often in an encounter group we have heard one member say, "Were you angry when I refused to answer your question?" and the other member responded, "I'm really sorry, but I must admit I didn't notice that you didn't answer it. Something else must have happened about that time—but, no, I wasn't angry."

Although clues are subject to error, if we keep in mind their tenuous value, we can often obtain good leads for further investigation. Upon occasion, direct questions following "obviously related responses" can suggest more valid inferences regarding how others see our behavior and how they feel about it. This is especially true when we say something intended to be funny and people look at us but nobody laughs. It is also significant when we overtly show we are distressed, emotionally upset, hurt or deeply angered—and nobody acts as if they care.[18] In such cases we should make sure that they have noticed our behavior before we conclude that no one cares about our feelings. Sometimes in a group other people are too busy worrying about their own troubles to have time to notice ours.

A most important clue to how we are being seen is provided when others refuse to "play our game." Your games and my games may be different, but most of us pursue some interaction ploys from time to time, even if we say, "Good morning," only in the hope of achieving a friendly climate with which to start a new day.[19] In reality, however, most of us play more serious interaction games. For example, consider the following case:

Joe: Hi. I wonder if I can talk to you a minute. The time for each of us to go on vacation is coming up in the meeting next Monday. I think we ought to give some kind of consideration to people who have been here longer.

Joan: I know that when we take our vacations is a problem.

Joe: You've been here a long time—longer than most of us. Don't you think longevity ought to be considered?

Joan: I really think we ought to give every one as equal a chance as possible. If longevity becomes a primary consideration, new people will be told when to go and have very little to say about it.

In this example, Joe can hardly conclude he was successfully dominating Joan. In addition, it is pretty obvious that he was seen as one attempting to exercise personal influence. He may still be unsure whether he was seen as somewhat friendly, neutral, or somewhat unfriendly, but on the dominant–submissive continuum he has a better clue regarding how he was seen.

Feedback

In chapter three we discussed feedback as a form of personal communication in which one person reports his perceptions of, and feelings about, another person's behavior. So that feedback may have optimal value we suggested adherence to a specific set of criteria which we identified as the openness paradigm: The person giving feedback describes his perceptions and feelings regarding an interaction experience previously shared with the other person; he owns these perceptions and feelings, and he reports the meaning he attributes to the shared experience, citing the exact incident as carefully as possible.

The above requirements for feedback are viewed as optimal although not often achieved. Much interpersonal behavior can be identified as feedback even though it does not meet these desired requirements. The nonverbal, nonvocal behavior of others in our presence can be viewed as feedback.[20] As we have suggested in the previous section of this chapter, such data provide only indirect and tenuous inferences. Their chief value lies in the provision of clues to be followed up by verbal questions or further observation. On the other hand, however, *clues have considerable value when they are inconsistent with or in contradiction to verbally reported perceptions.* If you are given oral feedback that you are seen as friendly, but the behavior of the other person seems to indicate that he views you as hostile, you should be very careful about accepting the report that you are seen as friendly.[21]

In addition to noting reports of how you are perceived and how others feel about these perceptions, you should listen carefully to the reports of *meanings others attribute* to your behavior.[22] For example, as a group starts a project, you may do your best to encourage a wide distribution of participation by the group members. You may sincerely feel you are contributing to democratic action on the part of the group. In a discussion of the way in which various members behaved as the group interacted, you may be told your behavior was "forceful" and "somewhat demanding." You may wisely wonder if this perceived behavior was admired, liked or resented. If you ask the group, you may be told that most of the members liked this behavior because they *understand you want all members to be given equal treatment* and achieve a share in the responsibility for the group decision. The point is this: *Perceptions, feelings, and meanings attributed to the perceived behavior* are all very important information.[23] Without each of these elements you will inadequately evaluate your interpersonal behavior. An error in evaluation can very possibly lead to inappropriate, needless destruction of some significant aspect of your self-image.

As we suggested in chapter three, the study of attribution of meaning to another's behavior has only just begun. We need to know far more about the ways in which a person attributes motives or intentions to another person. We should be especially careful that the motives or intentions we attribute to another person are not viewed by us as accomplished fact. Such inferences are extremely tenuous. But at this point we must also be very careful to look at the other side of the coin. *The meaning others attribute to our behavior is going to affect their responses to us.* Tenuous and inferential as it is, attributed meaning is going to color the way they see us and the motives and intentions they believe we have. *The world men create by their perceptions is the world to which they respond.* For each of us (for better or worse) there is no other world. Others respond to us on the basis of meanings that they attribute to our behavior because such attributions are all they have to work with. Thus, it is important to us to find out all we can about these attributions because they are very often subject to error and misinterpretation.[24] Once two teen-age brothers were discussing the attractive qualities of the girlfriend of one of them (Jerry). Jerry said she was so kind and thoughtful. His brother Jim said she was artificial, putting on an act to get Jerry to take her out. Jerry said he couldn't detect any "act." Finally, Jim said, "Well, like they say, what you see is what you get." Jerry quickly replied, "I know that's true—but what I see, I like; and I'm pretty happy to get it." We reaffirm the concept—what people see is what they get. We further assert that what they see is that to which they will respond.

Requests That We Change

We should always be wary of direct requests that we change our interpersonal behavior. We should try to obtain information regarding the perceptions and feelings underlying these requests. In fact, the nature of these perceptions and their interpretation should concern us much more than the request as such.

At no time should a person change his behavior simply because he is asked to do so. Rather, the decision to change should be a personal decision based upon the best possible information and feedback. Feedback should be evaluated in terms of probable openness or honesty of the feedback source, and should in all cases be checked out with more than one or two persons giving their perceptions and interpretations.

In numerous human relations laboratory groups a request for personal change may not be presented in a direct way but, rather, implied. Implicit requests may take the form of refusing to respond to us, perhaps by refusing to provide reinforcement of our behavior (for example, refusing to laugh at our humor or respond to our overtures of friendship). In these cases indirect requests or implications that we should change should be fully explored via responsible feedback on perceptions of us and interpretations of our behavior. Only when we are fully satisfied that we understand the nature of the feedback should we give careful consideration to the possible problems and potential values of change. At that point, we, as individuals, should make a decision for ourselves.

TYPES OF RELEVANT DATA

In our search for valuable information about our ability to relate to others we can obtain many items and bits of data. Feedback, to be valuable, necessarily must relate to discrete events, statements, or other particular items of our behavior. Even though this is done, we will still be hard pressed to interpret data and make sense out of the bits and pieces. We need focal points around which to organize discrete items of information. Although it may be valuable for us to learn that some particular mannerism, phraseology, or habit of ours causes irritation to others, a systematic integration of data is useful.

We suggest that the three basic elements of an interpersonal relationship presented in chapter four provide a useful frame of reference. As you perceive responses to your own behavior you can make inferences regarding your ability to become *involved* with others. As you receive verbal feedback you can detect indications of your desire to *dominate* others or your willingness to be *submissive*. As you respond to others you note your desire for *affection* along with your readiness to show *warmth* or *regard* for others.

In our work with encounter groups we have found it useful to encourage members to watch for data that tells them something about themselves regarding these three dimensions of interpersonal behavior:

1. Inclusiveness versus avoidance
2. Dominance versus submissiveness
3. Affection versus hostility.

It seems to us that trying to change one's behavior by adopting some specific act such as saying, "I like you," or "I like what you say," is artificial and is often viewed as a ploy or manipulative act. Adopting a general objective, such as trying to show more warmth, can lead to many different behaviors that are more spontaneous, genuine, and credible. Similarly, trying to *avoid* a certain behavior such as saying, "Well, here's what I think we should do," (frequently seen as attempting to dominate) is not easy. Trying to break a *specific little habit* can cause a person to stumble over words, hesitate, become frustrated. Resolving to pay more attention in general to what others want to do can produce many different, spontaneous behaviors viewed as genuine. In similar fashion, resolving to be more involved or more responsive in a general way can be fruitful in diminishing silent withdrawal or covert defensiveness.[25] We recommend consideration of these three dimensions for sorting out various items of feedback. We also suggest that one or another can be used as general behavior targets for changing one's interpersonal behavior.

ADVANTAGES OF DELIBERATE FEEDBACK

There are real advantages as well as dangers in the use of direct, deliberate, verbal feedback. Here we are concerned with feedback of an overt nature given by one person directly to another. Such feedback frequently occurs in encounter groups and is often encouraged by group leaders.[26]

Overt feedback can occur on one or more of three levels:

1. Perception: "I see you trying to get Mary involved in our discussion."
2. Attitude toward behavior perceived: "I like what you are trying to do."
3. Attributed motive (interpretation of behavior perceived): "I know you're trying to get all of us involved without anyone being left out."

To be most valuable to another person, feedback should be given to him directly and in terms he can understand. It should identify his behavior specifically, and should be offered as soon as possible after that behavior has occurred.[27]

We have identified at least four advantages of such overt feedback: Opportunity to elicit explanation and review of feedback; a chance for illusions to be challenged; the possibility that alternative behaviors will be suggested; and the likelihood that support for attempted change will be mobilized.

Opportunity to Elicit Explanation

Although deliberate, direct feedback may be given in terms that seem to be clear, frequently it is not easily understood by the recipient. Part of one's inability to understand may be due to anxiety, temporary embarrassment, defensive mechanisms or habits, or even personal hostility toward the individual feedback giver. Even so, direct verbal feedback creates the opportunity to raise questions, ask for illustrations or citation of specific events. When it occurs in a group it provides opportunity to ask others for their opinion as a form of check on its validity. In this way direct verbal feedback has considerable advantage over simply observing the ways in which others respond to us and then inferring a relationship between one's behavior and the responses observed. As a matter of fact, direct verbal feedback can be requested as a check on such inferences.[28]

Perspective on Illusions

Many of us seem to operate under various illusions about ourselves and the ways others are responding to us.[29] These illusions, of course, are built upon our hopes or fears, and they can become fairly real to us. Many television dramas are based on the comical behavior of a character who takes seriously an illusion about himself that is clearly discernible as unreal to all others with whom he interacts.

Direct feedback from others who are honest can often challenge self-delusion. As our illusions are challenged, we once again search for reality. Reconsideration of our illusions can be a valid step toward personal growth.[30]

Identification of Possible Alternatives

Direct verbal feedback creates the opportunity for the recipient to stop, listen, and think. He is invited to review his behavior and reconsider its merit. Implicitly he is asked to consider possible change.

This invitation should be implied rather than demanded. The simple act of feedback should only invite consideration of change. However, possible changes and various alternatives can be discussed by the feedback giver and receiver. It should be remembered that suggested alternatives may be positive rather than negative; they may encourage doing more of what is already being done—being supportive of others or showing warmth and friendliness. Implied change need not always involve stopping undesirable behavior.

Mobilization of Support for Attempted Change

As confrontive feedback is provided, it should be presented in a way that shows genuine concern and regard for the person to whom it is given. At no time should a leader or any other group member attempt to change a person; rather, they should try to create a situation in which it is possible for him to change if he wants to do so.

When interest in possible change is shown by the feedback receiver, he can be encouraged by other group members. Group support for attempted changes can be requested and encouraged by the leader or by group members.[31] This support can be of real value; it can demonstrate a climate of acceptance of an attempt to change even though this attempt may be awkward or unsuccessful.

PROBLEMS INHERENT
IN THE FEEDBACK PROCESS

We have suggested specific values of direct feedback. Along with these advantages are inherent problems which must be anticipated and counteracted. They are essentially two-fold: perceptual and motivational.

Perceptual Filters and Biases

Direct feedback from one member of a group to another is useful to the extent that the feedback giver's perceptions of the recipient's behaviors are accurate. Such perceptions are always subject to distortion based upon the background of the perceiving person. We see what we expect to see. Our experience and background alerts us to see or notice some things and fail to see others.[32]

Our interests as well as our fears—those things which threaten us —tend to make us selective in noticing or ignoring various elements within our perceptual field.[33] At no time should one person's report of his perception of another person be taken as precisely accurate and complete.

In many cases the language in which feedback is given additionally reflects the biases of the feedback giver. Often it reflects his own fears or prejudices. In many cases the language used carries more of an indication of the frame of reference of the feedback giver than a true reflection of the recipient's behavior.[34]

In receiving feedback, the recipient should be aware of these inherent problems of restriction, selection, and distortion. As he hears feedback on how he is perceived by others, this principle should be kept in mind: What *they* see is what *you* get.

Motives of the Feedback Giver

For feedback to be valuable the feedback giver must be honest. Even if this is the case, the feedback will be subject to the *perceptual* problems indicated above. This problem of lack of honesty can be diminished somewhat if the feedback giver is willing to recognize some of his own personal biases and fears, suggesting possible elements of perceptual error. In order to give this kind of information along with his feedback, he must be exceptionally open and honest as a person. The appropriate motivation in giving feedback is a desire to be of help or value to the other person. There should be willingness to recognize his wishes or desires. In addition, the feedback giver should consider the recipient's current emotional state.[35]

The feedback recipient should be constantly aware of possible motives of the feedback giver that are less than optimal. There may be personal jealousy; the feedback giver may envy the status or ability of the recipient. Some feedback givers are motivated by the simple desire to focus attention upon others, thus avoiding criticism of their own behavior. In some groups, on rare occasions, there may be a person who enjoys malicious attack upon another person and takes sadistic delight in seeing someone burn or squirm.[36] Such people can find their way into human relations training groups and their motives should be identified and exposed whenever possible.

Ways of Counteracting Feedback Problems

The perceptual and motivational problems described above are inherent in the process of giving direct interpersonal feedback. They are limitations that must be recognized and counteracted. When they appear to be operating to a very high degree, that is, when feedback appears to be unreal—based on personal projections or fantasy, or dishonest, or based upon ulterior motives of the feedback giver—the process of giving direct feedback should be stopped and these problems discussed by the group. Any group member, on perceiving these conditions, can call them to the attention of the group. These perceptions, of course, are subject to the same limitations and errors described above; however, if they are openly discussed and reviewed by the other members of the group, there is less likelihood of distortion being undetected.

The best safeguard against erroneous or dishonest feedback is to have it occur in a group rather than a dyad. There is some "safety in numbers." This principle is especially valid if the group has considered the importance of personal feedback and, as a group, are committed to giving one another the most accurate and honest feedback possible. This is an extremely commendable group goal, and commitment may be hard to obtain and even more difficult to implement. Even so, as we see it, it is the primary objective of human relations training groups, and without it, groups will be of slight value and may do great personal harm.[38]

So far as we can discern there is no way in which a group can completely eliminate the perceptual and motivational problems inherent in the feedback process. However, our observation and experience with people indicates that generally they would rather give accurate and honest perceptions than erroneous or malicious distortion. In essence, we believe that most people would rather help than harm others. Deliberate attention to these problems on the part of a training group can significantly enhance the group members' efforts to achieve this purpose.[38] In this domain the leader of the group carries special (but not sole) responsibility.

In a large study of the effectiveness of human relations training groups at Stanford University in 1969, Morton Lieberman reported significant data on the effect of leader behavior regarding methods of giving or encouraging personal feedback. Leaders who were the most confrontive provided the most intense emotional stimulation, produced a few high learners and moderate changes, but also the highest number of dropouts and "casualties"—severe personality disturbance, severe depression, or psychotic breaks. Leaders who did no confronting and did not encourage it produced almost no positive outcomes and, in fact, very few negative ones—participants with these leaders remained relatively unaffected by the training experience.[39]

The study also showed that the most effective leaders were those who specialized in (1) caring and (2) interpreting interpersonal behavior. They demonstrated to observers that they personally cared for the participants; group members perceived them as giving warmth and love. These leaders attributed meaning to interpersonal behavior by clarifying or interpreting group members' interactions. In giving these interpretations they provided personal feedback, translating their own feelings and perceptions into terms understandable by the group members. In addition to showing care and providing interpretations of members' experiences, they also used moderate stimulation of member participation in the group and occasionally gave attention to "house-keeping" functions such as managing use of time and suggesting procedural norms or rules.

A leader who confronts without caring is dangerous. He should be stopped by alert group members. He is an accident (or casualty) looking for a place to happen. Conversely, a leader who cares but never gives confrontive feedback is not likely to produce any significant learning for the group members. Optimum benefits are most likely to be produced by leaders who care and, in addition, provide personal feedback that gives meaning to the interpersonal experience of the group members. Lieberman characterizes these leaders as follows:

> These were individually focused leaders who gave love as well as information and ideas about how to change. They exuded a quality of enlightened paternalism; they were good daddies; they subscribed to some systematic theory about how individuals learn which they used in the group, but which they did not press.[40]

DANGERS TO BE AVOIDED

We have suggested certain problems inherent in the feedback process and the special responsibility carried by leaders of training groups. In addition to these factors, there are certain other dangers that must be avoided if group members are to engage in a feedback process which provides individuals with confrontive data that may disconfirm or disturb their images of themselves. As we have said earlier, the essential element of confrontation takes place in the mind of the person receiving new data that conflict with his *a priori* self-perception. There are at least three conditions under which this can be dangerous in the sense that it may be severely disturbing and possibly lead to psychological damage. We will look at each one in detail in this section.

Psychological State of the Confronted Person

If a group member is led to expect that he will meet with others for mild, friendly, but impersonal interaction and is suddenly confronted by personal data that contradict his self-image, the shock is likely to counteract any valuable benefits. If personal feedback violates his expectations or "psychological set," he is not likely to be able to evaluate it in a useful, reflective way.[41] On the other hand, if feedback is the norm of the group, the member may be able to use it. This will be true, however, only if he is not at that time in a heightened condition of emotional arousal.[42] If he is severely upset, frightened, anxious, or violently angry, feedback at that time will be of slight value.

Feedback, to be of optimal use, should be expected (preferably requested) by the person receiving it. It should be the normal work of the group, and the receiver should be in an emotional state such that he can give it careful consideration. If group members persist in giving an individual feedback when these psychological conditions are not present, there is real danger that severe psychological disturbance may result. In such cases encounter group leaders and other responsible group members should request that feedback be delayed until conditions are satisfied—in fact, they should insist that this danger be avoided. Discussion of this danger by the group members can help to provide appropriate psychological conditions by properly preparing group members for personal interaction.[43]

Lack of Group Climate of Support

It is not enough simply to have a group interacting and giving personal feedback for feedback to be useful to the members. In fact, without a group climate of mutual support personal feedback can be psychologically harmful.[44] A supportive climate is one in which members are accepted as they are, not necessarily for *what* they are, but for their *potential*. They are capable of empathy for others, genuine behavior that is not artificial or manipulative, and feelings of regard, affection, and love.

To the extent that these capacities are not demonstrated by the group, its members may undergo personal psychological strain if direct personal feedback is presented. On the other hand, if empathy, warmth, and genuineness are demonstrated by the group, the stress of accepting confrontive data can be more easily borne by feedback recipients.[45]

The danger of excessive individual stress from personal confrontive feedback in a cold malicious group is real and important. It should be avoided by responsible leaders and group members. Any feedback target should be asked whether or not he feels that there is an adequately supportive group climate. Adequacy should be judged by each individual feedback recipient at the time feedback is being given, and his definition of it should be respected by other group members. Only in this way can an appropriate degree of supportive climate be ensured.

Relationship Between Feedback Giver and Receiver

The interpersonal relationship between the person presenting confrontive data and the recipient of such data is exceedingly important in terms of hostility versus warmth and dominance versus submission. The relationship should be one of mutual respect. Of course, feedback can be of additional benefit if there is a feeling of mutual warmth and affection. A real limitation exists if the recipient believes that the feedback giver holds an attitude of hostility toward him. Personal communication involving confrontive data is a very sensitive matter; if the information source is viewed as personally hostile or violently angry, the data will be viewed with suspicion of malice and possible distortion. The real danger here is that even accurate feedback may be distorted in the perception of the receiver.[46]

Feedback under conditions of personal hostility on the part of the giver *as perceived by the receiver* should be discouraged by a responsible leader or member of a training group. When such feedback is offered, all responsible persons should ascertain that the receiver perceives no hostility on the part of the feedback source. If hostility is so perceived, the two persons involved should discuss the hostility before feedback is given.

The three dangers suggested above—inappropriate psychological state of feedback receiver, poor climate of group support, and perceived hostility of feedback giver in the view of the receiver—are extremely important. They should be given careful consideration by the members of a training group. We view the provision of feedback as the essential and most important work of a group. Personal communication is the very essence of human relations laboratory training. For this work to be beneficial, these three dangers must be considered and, when present in a group, they should be handled as preliminary work if the real work of the group is to go forward.

RESPONDING TO CONFRONTIVE FEEDBACK

In this section we will be concerned with ways in which a feedback recipient can make optimal use of the opportunity to receive and use it.

Inviting Feedback Before It Is Offered

It is much easier to analyze and to evaluate feedback if you have asked for it instead of having it thrust upon you. In terms of your attitude you can "get set" for it; in such cases your emotional response is less likely to get in the way of your careful listening and appropriate understanding.[47]

You can also help to direct feedback into areas of most importance to you if you request that it refer to specific behaviors. Look at the following case as an example:

Laurie: In our review of our work on yesterday's project some mention was made of domination of other members of the group. I would like to ask for feedback on my behavior including any perceptions of me as dominating the group.

Randy: I was somewhat irritated because I felt you cut me off when I was explaining my idea for implementing our plan of action.

Laurie: I guess I didn't realize I was cutting you off. I didn't intend to do that.

Trudy: Yes, I noticed that you cut him off. You were trying to get us to finish our discussion by 4:00, and he never did get to tell us what he had in mind.

Laurie: I'm not very considerate of others' ideas sometimes.

Randy: The group finally decided to do about the same as I had in mind, but I felt you kept me from suggesting my idea.

Laurie: I'll try to be more considerate in the future.

Randy: Oh, that's okay.

Laurie: Has anyone noticed other ways in which I seem to dominate the group?

Trudy: Sometimes you repeat someone else's idea and ask us to comment on it. Why don't you let them ask for comments on their own ideas?

In a case like this it is quite likely that discussion will continue with various members offering additional feedback. The recipient can thus provide guidance into the area of most concern at that time.

Accepting Invitations to Receive Feedback

Occasionally a group member may be invited to consider hearing feedback. Easy acceptance of such an invitation can encourage openness of feedback regarding perceptions of others and their feelings about these perceptions. Ready acceptance of such an invitation tends *to reduce anxiety and tension on the part of feedback givers,* making their task easier and the quality of the feedback thus more dependable.[48]

Participating in the Feedback Process

An attempt on the part of the feedback recipient to empathize with the feedback giver can enhance the quality of the feedback process. An attempt to see things from his point of view, to "walk in his shoes," can assist the recipient in his understanding the feedback offered. This is particularly beneficial regarding an assessment of the *feelings* of the feedback giver by the feedback recipient. It is also very helpful in gaining an *interpretation of the motives* of the feedback giver.[49] Insight regarding these feelings and motives can be very useful in gaining an appropriate understanding of the feedback. It can also help the recipient to assess properly the validity of the feedback source's perception. It can be especially helpful to the recipient if his image of himself is contradicted, and an implicit invitation to change behavior is thus presented.

The value of feedback can be enhanced by the recipient's direct participation in the feedback process, which can take the form of questions designed to clarify the feedback offered. The following example illustrates this principle:

Ned: You say you feel I am supportive of other members of the group when they seem to be having difficulty, but that essentially you see me as a "cool" person who does not get very excited.

Mark: Yes, you don't show a lot of emotion. You don't cry or throw your arms around people.

Ned: Do you feel I am too cold? That I am sometimes insensitive to the feelings of others?

Mark: No, as I said, I feel you are supportive of the others when they need you. You show that you appreciate their feelings. You seem to be strong and steady when others are in trouble. To me you are a strong person.

Ned: Cool but not cold?

Mark: Yes.

Ned: Strong but not insensitive?

Mark: Yes.

Ned: In any of these perceptions do you have any negative feelings? Any that bother you or make you dislike me? I'm particularly interested in hearing what I do that I shouldn't do—or what I don't do that I should.

Mark: Well, there is one thing, I guess. You sometimes seem to give me the feeling that you are ready to help people but you don't like to see them cry. I have the feeling that you don't like "whiners" and that crying is pretty much like whining.

Ned: Do you feel I am not supportive of persons who feel sorry but aren't doing anything much to help their situation?

Mark: Yes, that's a good way of putting it.

Ned: I think that's a fairly accurate perception. I tend to see myself pretty much that way. Does this bother you—make you feel that I might sometimes be less than a good friend, perhaps in some way let you down?

Mark: Yes, sometimes I get that kind of an impression and it bothers me a little.

Ned: I really do appreciate your openness in your comments. I'd like to check this out with some of the other members of the group.

Resisting Old Habits in Responding to New Data

Many times we respond to new self-confrontive data in a defensive manner. Sometimes in order to reduce our inner conflict—our "cognitive dissonance"—we tend to derogate the source. Occasionally we distort our perception of the data or interpret it in ways that are more consistent with prior information and our prior self-image.[50] Any tendency to respond in defensive ways should be considered by the feedback recipient.

Old habits, well-entrenched, are very difficult to set aside. Even so, an effort should be made. Factors that can be of assistance in this effort may be a supportive climate in the group, behavior of a leader or another member of the group who can serve as a desirable model, and a sincere desire on the part of the recipient to learn as much as possible about his own interpersonal behavior.[51]

Accepting Feelings of Others as Facts

Sometimes when a person tells us how he feels about our behavior it is difficult for us to accept the statements as facts. We hear them as *evaluations* of us rather than as *reports of their feelings*. We tend to see feelings of others as *our* responsibility rather than *theirs*. Sometimes we wonder how they can feel the way they do when we have done "nothing" to generate these feelings about us.

The point to be made here is that a report of how a person feels about us is subjective data, available in actuality only to that person in his own mind or nervous system. While it is true that we can make a judgment or inference regarding how he feels about us by noting his behavior in our presence—for example, how he responds to us— if we believe a person to be honest and if we can see no behavior that leads us to doubt his word, we must accept for the most part, his report of his feelings as fact.

Accepting another person's feelings as fact does not necessarily obligate us in any way to be responsible for these feelings. His perceptions of us are subject to all of the limiting or distorting influences we have previously described. He may feel toward us the way he does as a result of some irrational influence—we may remind him of a domineering father, a hated teacher, or a malicious neighbor. He may be entirely unconscious of identifying us with a hostile acquaintance in his past. To a very large extent, a person's feelings about another person should be viewed as his own responsibility rather than the responsibility of the person toward whom he holds an attitude.

We do not mean to suggest that we should show no consideration for the way other people feel toward us—indeed, we should. Rather, we are suggesting that we should accept their statements as fact if we have no reason to doubt their honesty. Then we can consider how our behavior may be related to those feelings. This approach can assist us in reducing our defensiveness and can provide considerable help in evaluating the importance of feedback.[52]

Discouraging Irresponsible Confrontation

As we accept feedback of confrontive information we should seek to reduce our defensiveness and try to understand how others see us and why they might feel the way they do. This does not mean that we should accept or encourage irresponsible confrontation. In fact, we should discourage it.

Irresponsible confrontation occurs when feedback is presented regardless of the psychological state of the recipient. It also occurs when the relationship between the feedback giver and receiver is poor. In a very general way it is irresponsible when the recipient has not asked for it or if, in some way—verbally or nonverbally—he has indicated that he can't handle it at that time. If one is offered feedback under these conditions, he should discourage it at that time. Responsible members of the group should support this stand, but should also encourage the person to try to seek useful feedback at a more appropriate time.

Irresponsible feedback can be a waste of time. Of even greater importance, it can be psychologically harmful. Although there appears to be little scientific evidence of severe psychological damage caused by confrontation, damage is clearly possible when anxiety is introduced by confrontive data. To be effective as a learning device, confrontation must disrupt the recipient's cognitive system, particularly that part of it which relates to his image of himself. In this way confrontation ordinarily produces at least some degree of temporary disorganization of the confronted person's self-image, but this disorganization can be an effective step in learning and self-improvement if it takes place in a group which provides a climate of support.[53]

PROTECTIONS TO BE EMPLOYED

Feedback of a personal nature should be encouraged in encounter groups because it is the very basis of learning about oneself in terms of interpersonal relations. When feedback is confrontive, that is, when it is contradictory to a preconceived self-image, anxiety will be a likely contingency.[54] Because confrontation by personal feedback can produce anxiety, certain protections should be employed: It should occur only in a group where a climate of interpersonal support is present, and care should be taken to preserve the feedback recipient's option to change or *not* to change.

Protection by the Group

Feedback of confrontive data should be presented in a group rather than in a dyadic or one-to-one situation for two reasons. The first is that the group members can act much like a jury in deciding the degree to which any item of feedback is valid. Any one member presenting feedback on any single item of behavior is subject to the biases and prejudice of distorted perception. Checking this out with the other members of a group can be a valuable protective measure.[55] The other reason for giving feedback in a group is that as anxiety is produced by the feedback giver, the other members of the group can provide a climate of support for the recipient. They can let him know that he is viewed as a valuable person; they can show that they care about his feelings and that his discomfort or anxiety is a matter of concern to them. This type of support can help to reduce defensiveness and increase the possibility of utilization of the confrontive feedback even if anxiety is present. This climate of support is just as important to learning in human relations laboratory groups as is the feedback process itself.[56]

Preservation of the Option Not to Change

When confrontive feedback is given, it is impossible to avoid the implication that the recipient's self-image should change. For this reason the recipient cannot avoid viewing this feedback as an invitation to consider changing his behavior. However, *if human relations training is to avoid the charge that it is manipulation, even similar to "brain washing," the option to choose not to change must be preserved.* This option of *not* changing can be preserved only by deliberate effort on the part of the group and the instructor or trainer. *Group support for choosing not to change should be as readily forthcoming as support for consideration of confrontive feedback with its implicit suggestion for change.* Group support for the not-changing option must be given deliberate attention and not left to chance.[57]

Once the recipient has been given confrontive feedback—once he has heard it and given it his careful consideration—his choice to change or not to change should be respected by the group. In this way particular emphasis should be placed on the behavior of the group leader or trainer. Leaders who, through high charisma or aggressive stimulation, put severe pressure on participants to change, tend to produce the greatest amount of psychological disturbance for the participants.[58] One way the leader can avoid this is to make serious attempts to preserve the participant's option *not* to change *if that is his choice.*

SUMMARY

In this chapter we have given special consideration to confrontive feedback in human relations training groups because it is both extremely valuable for personal learning and, at the same time, likely to produce at least moderate degrees of anxiety.

The dynamics of confrontation (as we have used this term) consist of a person receiving feedback that is at least in part contradictory to his current self-image. In essence, he confronts himself with this new information and reconsiders his image of himself. The recipient then considers his available options: Is a change possible? Would change produce a more desirable self-image? Would it improve the capability of relating to others? Would it be too difficult or too painful? When deliberation indicates that new behavior should be tried, its experimental or trial use is further evaluated. If desirable results occur, the new behavior is incorporated into the habitual behavioral repertoire of the feedback recipient.

Sources of confrontive data were identified as (1) our own perceptions of how we respond to others and how they respond to us, (2) deliberate feedback from others, and (3) overt requests that we try to change. The types of relevant data that can be confrontive are most likely to concern ways in which we show others that we wish (1) to be included or not included in their interactions, (2) to dominate or be dominated, and (3) to be affectionate or hostile or be treated with affection or hostility.

The advantages of the use of deliberate, overt feedback were identified as opportunities for (1) eliciting explanation, (2) gaining others' perceptions of our illusions, (3) identifying possible alternatives, and (4) mobilizing support for an attempted change of behavior.

Problems inherent in the feedback process were shown to be the perceptual filters and biases of the feedback giver, and his motivations. Dangers to be avoided in this process include an inappropriate (hyper-anxious) state of the feedback recipient, lack of a supportive group climate, and a tense or hostile relationship between the feedback giver and receiver.

The feedback recipient can increase the potential value of confrontive feedback by responding in certain ways. He can invite feedback and thus help to direct it into fruitful channels. He can readily accept invitations to receive feedback, thus reducing tension on the part of both giver and receiver. Participating in the feedback process can help to elicit feedback most immediately useful to the recipient. Resisting old habits of responding defensively to new personal information can elicit clearer and more useful data. Accepting the feelings of others as facts, even when they are reported as being directed toward oneself, can help one to see that such feelings are primarily the responsibility of the person holding such feelings rather than the responsibility of the person thus regarded. Accurate placing of responsibility can diminish defensive behavior and provide opportunity for greater utilization of personal feedback. Finally, the feedback recipient can and should discourage irresponsible confrontation when it is directed toward him.

Because the use of confrontive feedback in human relations training is so important for learning, it should be used; because anxiety is so likely to be a contingent factor, certain protections should be employed. Confrontive feedback should be given only in a group where individual interpersonal perceptions can be checked for validity, and a climate of group support can help to diminish the attendant personal anxiety. A very important additional protection is the deliberate attempt on the part of the group and leader or trainer to preserve the feedback recipient's option *to choose not to change* once the confrontive feedback has been received. Only by preservation of this option can an encounter group avoid the charge that it is a device for manipulation of people—"brainwashing" them or molding them into some preconceived, preferred social image.

8

tHE MATURE pERSON

Our modern culture tends to make us behave like machines, moving in routine monotony, separated from one another. We become alienated from each other and, ultimately, from ourselves. A common complaint is that there are very few real challenges, and no occasions that compel a person to extend himself—to grow to his utmost capacity. There is no demand to be heroic—no need for heroes.

Heroism in a frontier society required taking personal risk, courage to test one's ability, and perseverance in the face of difficult circumstances. Traditional heroism has usually involved a worthy cause, consideration of others, high devotion to a principle, and great personal integrity. In the ancient classics epic heroism lay in the development of the hero—his growth in experience and wisdom.

It appears to us that there still exists a great opportunity for personal heroism. Today's challenge lies in the area of growth and development in interpersonal relations. There is a tremendous challenge in the area of personal living. The quest for increased self-understanding and self-improvement can still be an adventure of heroic proportions.

In the development of one's ability to relate to other people, to understand one's own problems in working with others, and to learn how to enjoy the company of others, there is the challenge of personal risk. One must have courage and perseverance in the face of rebuffs and setbacks. There is also the element of a worthy cause, the opportunity to contribute to the lives of others, and to make their daily existence more pleasant and satisfying. In order to achieve these goals a person must be devoted to a great principle: the proposition that life today can be fulfilling, that we can find better ways of enjoying one another's company, and that alienation from self and others can be overcome. Devotion to this principle requires personal integrity when others refuse this challenge, accepting instead less taxing ways of dealing with the problem—"tripping out" with drugs, or senselessly sliding along the ruts of montonous existence.

Our purpose in his chapter is to present to you a challenge for adventure in understanding yourself and in increasing your ability to relate to other people. In viewing this challenge it is necessary to scan the interpersonal horizons of our culture, to look at the social influences that must be confronted and overcome. Most of us spend the bulk of our waking hours in the environment of a human organization—a school, a government agency, or an industry. These modern organizations pose severe obstacles to our achievement of the optimum potential for interpersonal relations. For this reason, as we attempt to challenge you to achieve this potential, we will also pay special attention to the obstacles posed by our social environment. Overcoming obstacles and achieving your interpersonal goals will require that you have personal courage, devotion to principle, perseverance, and integrity. Today, as in other ages, the need for heroism is great and the opportunity still exists.

THE INTERPERSONAL POTENTIAL

In our estimation three writers have had significant impact upon our thinking regarding the human potential for interpersonal relations: Abraham Maslow, Carl Rogers, and Erich Fromm. Other authors have made significant contributions, but these three stand out. To a large extent their contributions have been more philosophical than scientific, and this seems quite appropriate when considering the outer reaches of our potential for human relationships.

What people *can* do is to some extent a question that can be answered by empiric or scientific data if we may assume that studies have been made of a proper sample of people who really tried their very best, extended themselves to the limit. To date we have little evidence that such has been the case.[1] It appears that when people really try, they can do much more than anybody thought they could, and the optimum limits are not really known. On the other hand, the issue of what people *should* try to achieve in terms of optimum human relationships is essentially a philosophical question and cannot be answered by scientific means. In their writings, Maslow, Rogers, and Fromm have attempted to provide some answers.

Self-Actualizing, Relating, and Loving

In this book, *Toward a Psychology of Being*,[2] Abraham Maslow emphasized the importance of a person's effort to reach out, to dedicate himself, and to expect more of himself than ever before achieved. He believed that inside each of us is an inner core that is both instinctive and good in common moral terms, and that, if this core of motivation is encouraged and not suppressed, we can achieve self-actualization. That is, our inner self can be actualized. This process involves being aware of our inner selves, facing external realities as they are, and striving to achieve as our inner core so directs. In his writings Maslow had much to say about work, creativity, and a number of other human goals; however, in terms of our primary interest for the present chapter—The Human Relations Potential—he stressed love of being and love for others. As he saw it, when a person's inner self is encouraged to seek expression and achievement, he will fulfill his potential in a number of ways, one of which is to have a deep and abiding love for other people.

In many of his writings, particularly in *On Becoming a Person*,[3] Carl Rogers developed the concept of a fully functioning person. He emphasized personal growth through consideration of others and commitment to an interpersonal way of life that gives to others accurate empathy and unconditional regard while at the same time maintaining for the person a strong sense of his own genuineness.

Erich Fromm's *The Art of Loving*[4] stands out as a definitive statement of the nature of love in all of its various aspects—romantic, filial, brotherly, and erotic. He emphasized the importance of love of self and love of others. His primary theses were that a person must love himself to be able to love others, and that loving another person or persons is the only answer to the problem of human existence. Without the ability and opportunity to love someone else, one's life would be meaningless and of little value.

On the basis of our own sense of value and inspiration received from reading the works of Maslow, Rogers, and Fromm, we would like to challenge you to reach out toward others in ways that extend beyond all prior efforts—to transcend all prior images of yourself as you relate to other people.

Achieving Mature Human Relations

From time to time we have had our thinking challenged by the philosophical writings of others. Even so, we have devoted many hours to searching our own thoughts, writing phrases and paragraphs, and reviewing our sense of values. Out of this process we have developed our view of maturity in terms of interpersonal relations. We have often been intrigued by the emphasis on "personal growth and development" in the literature on human relations, and the very few clear statements of what a person is like or how he behaves when he has "grown and developed."

To our way of thinking a person who is mature in terms of human relations does the following:

1. Shows confidence in his ability to relate to others—shows trust of self and trust of others.
2. Readily tries new ways of relating to and working with others when old ways are inadequate.
3. Requests and listens to feedback from others regarding (a) how he is perceived and (b) how others feel about these perceptions; he uses this approach particularly when trying out new ways of relating to these others.
4. Evaluates this feedback, carefully discriminating between valid criticism and diatribe, prejudicial attack, or capricious comment.
5. Changes his behaviors with a minimum of tension or confusion *when he chooses to change.*
6. Demonstrates accurate empathy and nonpossessive warmth toward others.
7. Behaves in overt ways that are congruent with his inner feelings.

As you can readily see, our view of the mature person is not in terms of personality dimensions or overt behavior patterns so much as it is in terms of *mastery of a process* by which he can relate to others, changing behaviors as necessary or appropriate. This process enables him to explore his own behavior and feelings; to express these feelings or thoughts without fear; to establish veridical exchange of ideas via personal communication; to evaluate his own behavior in response to feedback; to support the efforts of others to relate to him; and to achieve a personal sense of self-acceptance and well-being. In this way a mature person brings his perceived self and ideal self closer together. In addition, he increases his sensitivity to the interpersonal needs of others.[5]

To us, the optimum of personal growth in human relations is attained when a person has learned that he will not ordinarily lose self-esteem by self-disclosure and related feedback, but that the surest way to increase self-esteem is to request and evaluate feedback from a trusted person, making changes in interpersonal behavior when possible and desirable. In essence, the mature person is one who has learned to feel confident of his ability to achieve personal improvement by use of personal communication—self-disclosure followed by feedback. When one has mastered this process and is confident that he can employ it effectively, he has attained a high level of maturity in human relations.

THE INFLUENCE OF THE SOCIAL ENVIRONMENT

In this book we have attempted to portray a way of achieving better human relations. In addition, we have challenged you to try reaching this objective—to transcend all prior images of yourself relating to those around you. However, we would be derelict in our responsibility to you if we stopped at this point, failing to recognize the problem of reaching your goal in the social environment in which most of us live.

Study after study has shown achievement of human relations goals while in laboratory groups, followed by loss of permanent achievement in the face of organizational influences "back home."[6] For this reason we will pay special attention to factors influencing interpersonal relations in the ordinary organization, the nature of a "healthy" organization in which human relations are given special consideration, and ways in which an organization can be changed or improved.

Interpersonal Relations in a Modern Organization

Organizations, both in theory and in undeniable, pervasive reality, constitute a tribute to our exquisite skill in social engineering and a demonstration of our capacity to create brittle asylums of interpersonal lunacy. Large bureaucratic organizations are constantly criticized for their inhumanity and impersonality. Universities, as well as other commercial and governmental organizations, are often guilty of reducing persons to numbers, computerizing interpersonal relationships, producing members obsessed with conformity, and contributing to anomie, anxiety, alcoholism, delinquency, ulcers, and wife-swapping. The bureaucrat relates to people in terms of his position; it is not to him as a person that respect is shown, but to his office. This replacement of person with position is the major characteristic of a large organization; it is as common as it is unhuman.[7]

In an established organization of large size and long duration certain practices relating to human relations are ordinarily found. They may appear to a greater or lesser degree, but will be overtly present in almost every case.[8] We shall discuss five such practices in this section.

Personal communication is restricted. In large organizations it is believed that important communication should be concerned with the organization's objective: providing a product or a service. Consequently, emphasis is placed on communication that is objective, without personal feelings. Members of the organization act as if their personal effectiveness will decrease if interpersonal relations are discussed. The keynote is, "Let's keep feelings out of our discussions." Members keep their interactions impersonal through use of informal suggestions and little penalties.

Personal problems are suppressed. Members learn to hide, suppress, and disown their interpersonal attitudes.[9] When a slip naturally occurs they may be heard to say, "I didn't really mean it to sound that way." They develop ways of keeping each other from discussing interpersonal problems, such as, "Let's not get into personalities." They have difficulty in handling situations where personal attitudes are expressed or implied; they worry, "I wonder what he meant by that?" They avoid consideration of new ideas that involve interpersonal relations. They tend to avoid any new idea that *might* involve human values, saying, "Let's not rock the boat." They avoid experimentation and exploration of new ideas that involve value judgments, saying, "Let's do it the safe way." Thus they become unaware of the impact of their feelings on others, sometimes saying to themselves, "I wonder why George acts as if I don't like him?" Interpersonal problems go unresolved; they tend to reoccur and increase over time.

Members become insensitive to interpersonal feelings and attitudes.
Not only are they insensitive to the impact of their interpersonal
attitudes on others, but poor at predicting the impact upon themselves of a show of feelings on the part of other persons.[10] Consequently, they often show the following behaviors:

Surprised confusion: "Why did she get sore?"
Frustration: "How can you talk to that guy?"
Heroic "objectivity": "Let's just look at the simple facts."
Mistrust: "You just can't rely on anybody anymore."

Safe interpersonal behaviors become the norm. Members discuss
mainly those ideas for which there is clear company or agency policy.
They tend to affirm values thought to be held by their superiors.
They give only tentative commitments to any direct question involving human values or a new, untested idea. Executives gather around
themselves employees whose communication behaviors are similar
to their own. Support for such superiors tends to lack commitment
on the part of their assistants.[11] There is little personal warmth,
regard, and trust.

Conformity, alienation, and anxiety abound. Presentation of technical information is substituted for discussion of personal problems.
Careful supervision and "sticking to the rules" replaces real attempts
at teamwork in making decisions. Policies are evaluated and revised
only in severe crises. At such times tension is very high and beneath-
the-surface emotion is intense. There is a general atmosphere of
distrust and quick defensiveness whenever personal problems or
interpersonal relations are involved.[12]

In these social environments it is difficult to implement the objectives of human relations training. Under such circumstances development of ways of relating to other people is discouraged. The
atmosphere is deplorable. In terms of individual growth and human
development, these organizations may properly be termed un-
healthy—even though they may make a profit or expand in size. As
a matter of fact, when they are large and profitable they are usually
poor as a climate for achieving one's personal goals in relating to
other people.[13]

A Healthy Organization

In terms of personal growth in human relations the essential elements of a social climate may be described. The following seven
conditions are requisite.

Change is expected.   To the extent that rigidity and conformity are the rule, individual interpersonal growth is handicapped. Reverence for tradition has some merit, but is debilitating if that tradition does not include exploration and innovation.[14]

Feedback is used.   Without the use of personal communication to provide a reflection of how one is perceived by others, awareness of need to change one's ways of relating to others is diminished. Feedback can motivate change, indicate type of change needed, and help one to evaluate attempts to achieve new behaviors.

Members are committed to each other.   When interpersonal commitment is present, a supportive climate assists a member in his explorative, innovative efforts. Although he may not easily achieve changes that are desirable or pleasing to others, he will be supported in his attempts. Included in this social climate will be a provision for a member to choose *not* to change. The interpersonal demand should be only that feedback be accepted and implied change be considered. Tolerance for individual differences in ways of relating to one another will be given as much respect as adherence to patterns usually thought to be pleasing. In essence, a mature person can tolerate individual differences in a climate where his needs are considered by others and his own individual peculiarities are tolerated.[15]

Decision making is shared.   Where those who are affected by a decision have some voice in its making, a healthier climate for personal growth and development exists. This does not mean that every decision is made by a committee. Rather, the thinking and desires of those persons affected by the decision will be explored, respected, and considered. In many cases they will be given a vote; in all cases they will have a voice. As this opportunity is extended, responsibility is incurred. As responsibility is assumed, a person grows in his self-image and in the esteem of others.[16] Growth, development, and maturity are thus related.

Personal growth is encouraged.   Leaders in the organization provide training and learning experiences for their assistants. In this way growth is encouraged. As additional responsibility is assumed and successfully shouldered, persons are rewarded. Within the organization is a pervasive feeling that there is always room at the top or at least the opportunity for advancement for people who grow and develop. Instead of griping about their situation, people are encouraged to do something about it, to take on greater responsibilities, to share in the task of improving their environment, and to become more capable individuals—both in terms of professional or occupational expertise as well as skill in relating to one another.[17]

Persons are open to each other and share confrontive information. In a healthy organization where members are personally committed to one another, that is, where a team spirit prevails, they can easily communicate with each other regarding their personal needs and attitudes. It is common practice and accepted behavior to provide one another with information of a confrontive nature—feedback that may or may not be in contradiction with one's self-image. This is done, of course, in a responsible manner. It is done when the individual wants it and can hear it and in a spirit of constructive sharing, not destructive malice. Reception, in turn, of similar feedback is expected. This particular practice of sharing interpersonal feedback is not easily achieved in most organizations.[18] Athletic teams where this practice has been achieved are outstanding examples of its usefulness. Although not easy to achieve, this particular practice is probably most important of all those discussed in this section; in essence, it is the most significant hallmark of a healthy organization.

Personal problems are discussed and resolved. When feedback is commonly shared, personal problems are commonly exposed and discussed. As a result of interpersonal commitment and a spirit of shared responsibility and teamwork, problems are resolved on a basis of mutual agreement or shared compromise. Although sometimes issues of interpersonal relations arise that one cannot afford to compromise, shared empathy and understanding usually provide a basis for bringing even these to a resolution that is mutually acceptable to the persons involved.[19]

Organizations in which these seven essential practices are common occurrences are, of course, rather rare. They do not happen by chance.[20] Achievement requires not only the efforts of top management but of most of the members of the organization as well. Suppose you are spending the majority of your waking hours in an organization where these conditions do not exist, but your reading and training in human relations leads you to wish they did exist. How can this situation be brought about?

The Process of Organizational Development

For at least thirty years human relations training groups have been striving to help individuals improve their ability to relate to one another.[21] In more recent years many persons professionally interested in this work have come to recognize that if the improvement an individual achieves in laboratory training is to be of optimal long-range use, the "back-home" environment in which he lives and works must be given careful attention. Efforts in this direction have been made by professionals in this area, especially those persons affiliated with the National Training Laboratory Institute for Applied Behavioral Science (commonly known in the field as NTL). Their experiments and practices have come to be known as Organizational Development (commonly referred to as OD).[22]

Efforts in organizational development (OD) ordinarily attempt to help an organization provide a better atmosphere for the development of optimum human relationships among its members. OD looks at the human side of organizational life and seeks to integrate individual needs for personal growth with organizational goals and objectives. A number of years of experiment, study, and evaluation have identified the essential requirements of this process.

Although we have stressed here the need for OD work and shown the type of organizational environment in need of its services, in this book we cannot hope to provide a detailed description of the procedure.[23]

In the following brief overview of the OD process we hope to provide the reader with a deeper appreciation of the type of effort required, along with rudimentary knowledge of the approach that may be taken. We wish, in essence, to expand an interested person's horizon, to release him from the notion that the only options available to a member of an unhealthy organization are to succumb to anomie, alienation, and isolation, or to leave the sinking ship. We want both to encourage such a person and to apprise him of the fact that organizational change is not easy, but requires extensive effort. For this reason we provide the following brief resumé of the OD process.

In an OD program the entire organization is involved. Although particular attention is paid to the upper echelons of management and, without exception, the support of top management is required, no part of the organization may be safely ignored.[24] Any single part of an organization may inadvertently affect any other part, and a subsystem left unexplored may, in the long run, defeat an OD effort. Likewise, all operations of the organization are concerned—not just social relations, for example, but task relations as well. For this reason, sensitivity training or laboratory group training of various parts of the organization will not be sufficient.[25] Who is responsible to whom may, in the final effort, be very important; also, expertise in performing a task may heavily influence the interpersonal relations of persons working together.[26] In an OD effort all parts and all phases of an organization are involved.

The entire human potential of the organization is reviewed. An attempt is made to mobilize the energy of the entire system. For this reason an "outside" consultant is usually required. There is no doubt that if an organization has members with appropriate experience and insight they could very likely conduct their own OD operation. As a matter of fact, the routine responsibilities of management should call for constant efforts in this direction. The primary argument in favor of use of a consultant is that on-site staff do not ordinarily succeed very well in achieving their own program. Very likely the reasons for this failure may include lack of full cooperation or support from top management. Also, a fresh view by an outsider can spot problems not quickly seen by persons "too familiar" with the organization. An additional reason, of course, may be lack of training and experience in implementing organizational change.[27] To mobilize the energy of an organization for self-improvement requires an ability to see human potential where it is often thought not to exist.[28] It involves a view of human beings as having human needs for responsibility and achievement. In the terms made popular by Douglas McGregor, "Theory Y" must be adopted, in which persons are viewed as wanting to carry responsibility and to achieve some work goals, without the need for constant coercion as exemplified in "Theory X."[29] Only by viewing persons from the former perspective can the full human potential of the organization be realized.[30]

Person-oriented objectives are adopted for the organization. This is not to say that objectives of profit, making a product, or providing a service are abandoned. However, objectives that will help members to be human beings instead of automatons are also identified and given a strong commitment.[31] They include the following:

1. To build interpersonal trust among individuals and groups.
2. To provide a sense of at least partial control of the organization by its employees.
3. To increase personal self-control and choice of personal goals by its members.
4. To create a climate of open, personal communication in the organization.

5. To achieve an appropriate functional balance between individual (or group) competition and cooperation.
6. To develop a system of rewards that recognizes achievement of (a) organizational needs (production, profit, etc.) and (b) human needs of its members.[32]

To achieve these goals, an operational program is set into motion. Ordinarily the first step is to collect data concerning the organization and its members. Diagnostic information is obtained through observation and interviews with as many members as possible. Some fairly sophisticated data-collection scales have been developed for this purpose. As data are collected, feedback (with individual personal sources unidentified) is continuously given to all members and groups in the organization.[33] Organizational changes and training programs are planned only after data gathering, feedback and responding to feedback have occurred. Individual members' viewpoints are solicited in planning of training programs as well as planning changes in organizational procedure or personnel.[34] Team building efforts are usually instituted; these projects ordinarily involve experiential learning in problem solving as well as increased competence in interpersonal relationships. Groups frequently work on developing personal competence in communicating, making decisions, solving problems, and meeting individuals' needs to be treated as human beings. For these training experiences actual problems and events existing in the organization are used. Laboratory group training in human relations is often (but not always) used to support efforts at team building and improvement of human relations in the organization.[35] Usually (but not always) an "outside" consultant is employed to manage this operation. He must work closely with top management but not become their "tool." In effect, he must see that a proper OD program is implemented, but he will be unable to do so if opposed significantly by persons in authority positions in the organization.[36]

An OD program can be an exciting experience. Like laboratory group training in human relations, it can uncover severe problems, encounter unexpected crises, demand high commitment and dedication, and if conducted well, achieve satisfying results.

THE URGENCY OF MATURITY

In this chapter we have been using the term *maturity* in a special sense: the ability to request, obtain, and use personal feedback in order to improve our capacity to relate to others in ways that satisfy us and them. We recognize fully that this objective is somewhat idealistic, and that probably not every person can achieve it completely. Nevertheless, visionary as it may be, it is an achievement sorely needed.

Desperation in a Land of Plenty

For a long time America has been known as a land of plenty. We are aware that we are living in an affluent society. Our technical knowledge and organizational skill is world famous. One would think that in this environment the individual would have reached the peak of human happiness. Such is not the case.

Our society is flooded with complaints about the computerized environment and a person's feeling of impotence and powerlessness in the face of it. We are perplexed by the emergence of vast, dense urban agglomerations—what in Dallas is called the "megalopolis"—with their crushing crowds of strangers and a feeling of loneliness in the presence of thousands of people like us. Despite the efforts of urban planners and social engineers there are severe complaints regarding the loss of individual privacy and a degraded sense of personal worth.[37]

In industry the subordination of workers to the requirements of machines has threatened to turn people into things, giving them a sense of being very unimportant in the face of their environment. The assembly-line worker is isolated and alienated from his fellow workmen; he is robbed of the minimal pleasure of interaction with a small, informal work group. In essence, individual isolation, anomie, and the break-up of community are the distinguishing features of our modern society.[38]

Our major concern in this analysis of our social environment is the pervasive image of men and women. Our culture tends to view a person as a stimulus–response mechanism, an abstract point of intersection between environment and response.[39] In industry people are viewed as an economic resource, something to be "managed" by "management." Employers, government planners, and social engineers, even though motivated at times by humanistic philosophies, tend to see persons as entities to be steered by socially manipulated rewards or punishments.[40] According to this image of the human being, laws of interpersonal behavior can be derived from rigorous studies of hungry rats pressing levers in small, dark boxes. Even in our schools and colleges numbers are assigned to millions of persons denoting their aptitude or ability, with little regard for the potential effect on their dignity, self-image, or practical fate.

We do not mean to say that there are not sensible employers and teachers throughout the country who see and treat their employees or students as human beings with personal needs, frailties, limitations, and quirks. Many times these personal characteristics are recognized as important. But, in essence, such recognition of them is primarily *as limitations on worker effectiveness* and problems that must be faced if the more important goals of productivity or profit are to be achieved. This recognition, valuable as it may be, does not significantly diminish the pervasive process in our culture of stripping individuals of their humanness, reducing them to objects instead of persons.

Where, in all of this desperate situation, is the mature person— open to feedback, ready to use it, willing to consider personal change in ways of relating to others? In the previous section of this chapter we described a type of program for environmental change called organizational development. We have implicitly held out some hope that efforts in that direction might help to turn the tide of dehumanization of men and women in our society. How far have these efforts been extended?

In a report of OD activities an ardent practitioner in the field has indicated that nearly fifty organizations have made significant efforts in this direction.[41] Some of these were large and some small companies. This achievement involves fewer than one out of every thirty thousand of the million and a half organizations in our country. The very great majority continue to manage the daylights out of their people; consideration of personal human growth and development is viewed as a luxury or frill, to be given serious thought only when time and profits are very plentiful.

In the face of this pervasive cultural climate, the man or woman who has been stripped of his or her sense of personal worth—isolated, insulated, and alienated—in desperation responds to the call for the formation of a training group designed to improve abilities (opportunities?) to relate to people. Those of us who work in the areas of interpersonal communication and human relations cannot afford to treat this need lightly.

The Human Potential

It is exceedingly difficult to behave in a mature way when surrounded by persons who are immature in terms of interpersonal behavior. Even very mature persons have a tendency to respond to children as children. To achieve and maintain a practice of mature interpersonal behavior requires continued commitment and revitalization.[42]

In the past (and to some extent in our present society) an increased openness to others could entail serious risk. The warrior who stopped "to talk things over" could be slain. The hard worker stayed on the job, wasting little time getting acquainted with his fellow workers. The serious student remained at his desk and did not talk with his neighbor.

Growth in human relations can be risky, even threatening. To open oneself to feedback from others and to give serious consideration to possible change involving untried ways of relating to others can be somewhat frightening. It involves letting go of ego and merging with the deeper stream of humanity. It also involves letting go of self-protective mechanisms.

On the other hand, growth can be a very powerful means for understanding the people around us. In a world constantly threatened by thermonuclear violence, it is imperative that we do not neglect the potential for survival. The rise of individual alienation is a cultural fact. Severe communication gaps exist between groups, generations, social classes, and subcultures. A new emphasis on human values is essential.

The human potential for improving interpersonal relations appears to be almost unlimited. Long-range programs conducted by Jack and Lorraine Gibb have demonstrated that, with extensive laboratory group work, participants can achieve levels of rewarding interpersonal relationships not previously believed possible, neither by them, nor by observers, nor by their trainers.[43]

In a climate of trust, openness, feedback, and interpersonal consideration, persons tend to move toward becoming more expressive, more spontaneous, more flexible, and more considerate of others.[44] It is as if, given a decent chance, they inherently want to be kind rather than hurtful when with others.

It seems to us that a primary hallmark of a person who is mature in his way of relating to others is that he has learned that persons *as* persons are not frightening or harmful. When he meets another person as a person he need not fear. When a person *acting a role* meets another person *acting a role,* fear may be justified.[45] When a supervisor penalizes an employer, it is *role meeting role.* When a teacher punishes a student, it is *role acting against role.* When a dissenter faces a bigot, *role meets role.* But when I, in open honesty, meet you *as another person,* I really need not be afraid. Strong feelings may be present, angers and hurts may be deep; but when you and I can see each other as persons, show our humanness to one another, and establish contact in a personal but genuine way, the expression of our feelings will be cleansing and helpful, and we will psychologically come closer together. To know this—that I can be myself and not be afraid—is the hallmark of the mature person. Our world is in great need of mature persons.

SUMMARY

In this chapter we have presented a challenge to you, the reader, to transcend your former visions of yourself in terms of relating to other people. This challenge takes on meaning as we recognize that most of us spend the majority of our waking hours in the controlled environment of some organization—school, business, government agency, etc.

We have suggested that a person who has grown, developed, and reached a level of maturity in his ways of relating to others will have mastered the use of a *process:* the use of personal communication to express his own ideas and feelings; to derive personal feedback from others on how he is perceived and how they feel about these perceptions; and to change his ways of relating to others when it is clear that changes will produce more satisfactory relationships.

Mature behavior is not ordinarily easy in our culture because of social influences. In an established organization the bureaucrat will relate to you in terms of his position rather than as person to person. When you are treated as a "student" or an "employee" by someone aware of his role as "teacher" or "manager," you can begin to feel the chill effects of a cold, inhuman organization.

In established organizations in our culture we have noted these practices:

1. Personal communication is restricted.
2. Personal problems are suppressed.
3. Members are insensitive to interpersonal feelings and attitudes.
4. "Safe," distrustful interpersonal behaviors become the norm.
5. Conformity, alienation, and anxiety abound.

In an organization in which healthy human relations exist we have noted seven conditions (such healthy organizations are quite rare):

1. Change is expected, not feared.
2. Interpersonal feedback is used.

3. Members are committed to each other.
4. Decision making is shared.
5. Personal growth of members is encouraged.
6. Persons are open and share self-confrontive information.
7. Personal problems are discussed and resolved.

In recent years efforts have been made to counteract the un-healthy patterns of behavior in organizations. A type of program called Organizational Development (OD) has been used in a few places. OD ordinarily involves these measures:

1. The entire organization is involved.
2. Its entire human potential is surveyed.
3. Person-oriented objectives are identified and adopted.
4. An operational program is set into motion to implement these objectives.

In the latter portion of this chapter we have noted the rise of loneliness and personal alienation in the midst of a land of economic and technological plenty. We have suggested that a primary cause of this problem is a pervasive image of men and women as things—economic resources to be used, factors to be manipulated in economic or social planning, entities that can be reduced to numbers, analyzed by digital computers, and manipulated like hungry rats in small, dark boxes.

In the face of this pervasive cultural climate we have pointed to the mature person as one who is not afraid to establish strong personal ties with other people even though social influences may not be favorable. He is open to feedback from others and gives serious consideration to possible change involving untried ways of relating to others. Such a person knows—is confident and shows this confidence—that if he openly meets and treats others as persons, not as things, if he shows humanness toward others and establishes contact in a personal but genuine way, he really has nothing to fear.

NOTES

CHAPTER 1

1. Carl R. Rogers, *Carl Rogers on Encounter Groups* (New York: Harper and Row, 1970), p. 131. A report of a participant on the impact of the encounter group experience.

2. Ibid.

3. Charles Schulz, "Peanuts," © 1969 by United Features Syndicate, Inc.

4. Max Birnbaum, "Sense About Sensitivity Training," *Saturday Review*, November 15, 1969, p. 82.

5. Gerard Egan, *Encounter: Group Processes for Interpersonal Growth* (Belmont, California: Brooks/Cole, 1970), pp. 5–9.

6. Jack R. Gibb, "The Effects of Human Relations Training," in Allen E. Bergin and Sol L. Garfield (eds.), *Handbook of Psychotherapy and Behavior Change* (New York: Wiley, 1971), p. 840.

7. William S. Latta, William F. Hummel, Jr., Sebastian Streifel, John S. Morrison III, and Jim L. Olsen, "Human Relations Training in the Army" (paper read at the Annual Current Trends in Army Medical Department Psychology conference, December 1–5, 1969, Denver, and published by the Office of the Surgeon General, Department of the Army, Washington, D. C.), p. 174.

8. Ibid., p. 173.

9. Rogers, *On Encounter Groups*, pp. 4–5.

10. Gibb, "Human Relations Training," pp. 851–52.

11. M. Duane Thomas, "Developing Human Potential Through Group Interaction: A Study of Changes in Personality Factors, Personal Attitudes, and Group Functioning in University Students Participating in Human Relations Training" (unpublished doctoral dissertation, University of Kansas, 1970), pp. 31–33.

12. Oasis Midwest Center for Human Potential, Summer 1973 Catalog, p. 2.

13. The forms of laboratory training listed by Rogers but omitted from these two groupings are sensory awareness, body awareness, body movement, creativity, Gestalt, and Synanon.

14. Rogers, *On Encounter Groups,* p. 5.

15. Egan, *Encounter,* p. 10.

16. Rogers, *On Encounter Groups,* p. 136.

17. Ibid., pp. 6–8.

18. John P. Campbell and Marvin D. Dunnette, "Effectiveness of T-group Experiences in Managerial Training and Development," *Psychological Bulletin* 70 (August 1968): 77.

19. Gibb, "Human Relations Training," pp. 841–42, 844.

20. Ibid., pp. 841–42.

21. Ibid., p. 855.

22. Campbell and Dunnette, "Effectiveness of T-group Experiences," pp. 98–99.

23. Edgar H. Schein and Warren G. Bennis, (eds.), *Personal and Organizational Change Through Group Methods: The Laboratory Approach* (New York: Wiley, 1965), pp. 215, 231.

24. Alan Hislop, "Company Men," *Saturday Review of the Arts* 1 (March 3, 1973): 70–71.

25. Associated Press dispatch, *Leavenworth* (Kansas) *Times,* June 28, 1972.

26. The entire issue of *Educational Leadership* for December 1970 was devoted to "Sensitivity Education: Problems and Promise."

CHAPTER 2

1. See chapters 1 and 2 in Bobby R. Patton and Kim Giffin, *Interpersonal Communication: Basic Text and Readings* for a detailed discussion of the varying perspectives on communication (New York: Harper and Row, 1974).

2. This section draws heavily on a paper, "Openness: Personalized Expression in Interpersonal Communication," by Joseph W. MacDoniels, Elaine Yarbrough, Claire L. Kuszmaul, and Kim Giffin, presented at the International Communication Association, April 1971.

3. Milton Rokeach, *The Open and Closed Mind* (New York: Basic Books, 1960).

4. Sidney M. Jourard, *The Transparent Self* (Princeton: Van Nostrand, 1964).

5. Barbara Long, Robert Ziller, and Ellen Henderson, "Developmental Changes in the Self Concept During Adolescence," *School Review* 76 (1968): 210–30.

6. Eleanor Maccoby, "Role-taking in Childhood and Its Consequences for Social Learning," *Child Development* 30 (1959): 239–52.

7. Kim Giffin and Kendall Bradley, "An Exploratory Study of Group Counseling for Speech Anxiety," *Journal of Clinical Psychology* 24 (1969): 98–101.

8. For a detailed discussion see Kim Giffin, "Social Alienation by Communication Denial," *Quarterly Journal of Speech* 56 (1970): 347–58.

CHAPTER 3

1. For a discussion of anxiety or apprehension associated with interpersonal communication see Kim Giffin and Bobby R. Patton, *Fundamentals of Interpersonal Communication* (New York: Harper and Row, 1971), pp. 165–76.

2. See Everett Shostrom, *Man, the Manipulator* (New York: Abingdon Press, 1967), pp. 11–15.

3. Such is not always the case, but at least three studies support the generalization: Jack R. Gibb, "Effects of Role Playing upon (a) Role Flexibility and upon (b) Ability to Conceptualize a New Role" (paper presented to the Annual Conference of The American Psychological Association, Cleveland, Ohio, 1953); Richard L. Burke and Warren G. Bennis, "Changes in Perception of Self and Others During Human Relations Training," *Human Relations* 14 (1961): 165–82; and Robert C. Carson and Martin Lakin, "Some Effects of Group Sensitivity Experience" (paper presented at the Meeting of The Southeastern Psychology Association, Miami Beach, Florida, 1963). For a careful review of related research findings see Jack R. Gibb, "The Effects of Human Relations Training," in Allen E. Bergin and Sol L. Garfield (eds.), *Handbook of Psychotherapy and Behavior Change* (New York: Wiley, 1971), pp. 839–61.

4. These three interpersonal needs were identified in a review of related research, as well as in additional research of his own, by William C. Schutz. See his *FIRO: A Three-Dimensional Theory of Interpersonal Behavior* (New York: Holt, Rinehart and Winston, 1958), pp. 13–56.

5. Leland P. Bradford, "Membership and the Learning Process," in Leland P. Bradford, Jack R. Gibb and Kenneth D. Benne (eds.), *T-Group Theory and Laboratory Method* (New York: Wiley, 1964), pp. 190–215; see especially p. 203.

6. W. Brandon Reddy, "Screening and Selection of Participants," in Solomon and Berzon (eds.), *New Perspectives on Encounter Groups,* pp. 53–67; see especially pp. 57–58.

7. Howard S. Becker, "Personal Change in Adult Life," *Sociometry* 27 (1964): 40–53.

8. Cf. Renato Tagiuri, "Person Perception," in Gardner Lindzey and Elliot Aronson (eds.), *The Handbook of Social Psychology,* 2d ed., Vol. III (1969): 395–499; see especially pp. 414–23.

9. Henri Tajfel, "Social and Cultural Factors in Perception," in Lindzey and Aronson (eds.), *The Handbook of Social Psychology,* pp. 315–94; see especially pp. 341–46.

10. Chester C. Bennett, "What Price Privacy," *American Psychologist* 22 (1967): 371–76.

11. Jack R. Gibb, "Sensitivity Training as a Medium for Personal Growth and Improved Interpersonal Relationships," *Interpersonal Development* 1 (1970): 6–31.

12. William H. Blanchard, "Encounter Group and Society," in Solomon and Berzon (eds.), *New Perspectives on Encounter Groups,* pp. 13–29.

13. Frederick H. Stoller, "A Stage for Trust," in Arthur Burton (ed.), *Encounter* (San Francisco: Jossey-Bass, 1970), pp. 81–96; see especially p. 90.

14. James Bebout and Barry Gordon, "The Value of Encounter," in Solomon and Berzon (eds.), *New Perspectives on Encounter Groups,* pp. 83–118; see especially pp. 94–105.

15. Edgar H. Schein and Warren G. Bennis (eds.), *Personal and Organizational Change Through Group Methods* (New York: Wiley, 1965); see pp. 17–18 and 41–42.

16. John W. Thibaut and Harold H. Kelley, *The Social Psychology of Groups* (New York, Wiley, 1959), p. 31. See also pp. 9–50.

17. George C. Homans, *Social Behavior: Its Elementary Forms* (New York: Harcourt, Brace, 1961).

18. For a summary and evaluation of these two theories see Marvin E. Shaw and Philip R. Costanzo, *Theories of Social Psychology* (New York: McGraw-Hill, 1970), pp. 69–103.

19. See Homans, *Social Behavior*, pp. 54–55; also see Thibaut and Kelley, *Social Psychology of Groups*, p. 20.

20. Thibaut and Kelley, *Social Psychology of Groups*, pp. 12–13.

21. Thomas A. Sebeok, "Animal Communication," *Science* 147 (1965): 1006–14.

22. Randall Harrison, "Nonverbal Communication," in Ithiel de Sola Pool, et al. (eds.), *Handbook of Communication* (Chicago: Rand-McNally, 1973).

23. Mark L. Knapp, *Nonverbal Communication in Human Interaction* (New York: Holt, Rinehart and Winston, 1972), pp. 8–18.

24. Lionel Tiger and Robin Fox, *The Imperial Animal* (New York: Holt, Rinehart and Winston, 1971), pp. 1–2, 6.

25. Homans, *Social Behavior*, pp. 57–61.

26. Thibaut and Kelley, *Social Psychology of Groups*, pp. 12–13.

27. Homans, *Social Behavior*, pp. 39–49.

28. Thibaut and Kelley, *Social Psychology of Groups*, p. 63.

29. Arnold Buchheimer and Sara C. Balogh, *The Counseling Relationship* (Chicago: Science Research Associates, 1961), pp. 109–11.

30. Warren G. Bennis, "Goals and Meta-Goals of Laboratory Training," *NTL Human Relations Training News* 6, No. 3 (1962): 1–4.

31. Sidney M. Jourard, "Healthy Personality and Self-Disclosure," *Mental Hygiene* 6 (1959): 1–12.

32. See Sidney M. Jourard, *Disclosing Man to Himself* (New York: Van Nostrand, 1968), pp. 40–48; also, Sidney M. Jourard, "Growing Awareness and the Awareness of Growth," in Herbert A. Otto and John Mann (eds.), *Ways of Growth* (New York: Grossman, 1968), pp. 1–15.

33. Daryl J. Bem, "Self-Perception Theory," in Leonard Berkowitz (ed.), *Advances in Experimental Social Psychology*, Volume 6 (New York: Academic Press, 1972), pp. 2–62; see especially pp. 2–8.

34. Ronald D. Laing, H. Phillipson, and A. R. Lee, *Interpersonal Perception* (New York: Stringer, 1966), pp. 9–22.

35. Carl R. Rogers, "The Process of the Basic Encounter Group," in James F. T. Bugental (ed.), *Challenges of Humanistic Psychology* (New York: McGraw-Hill, 1967), pp. 261–67; see especially pp. 268–69.

36. Jack R. Gibb, "Sensitivity Training as a Medium for Personal Growth and Improved Interpersonal Relationships," *Interpersonal Development* 1 (1970): 6–31; see especially pp. 21–25.

37. Herbert A. Otto, "Developing Family Strengths and Potential," in Herbert A. Otto and John Mann (eds.), *Ways of Growth* (New York: Grossman, 1968), pp. 81–90.

38. See Richard L. Burke and Warren G. Bennis, "Changes in Perception of Self and Others During Human Relations Training," *Human Relations* 14 (1961): 165–82; also,

Jack R. Gibb, "Meaning of the Small Group Experience," in Solomon and Berzon (eds.), *New Perspectives on Encounter Groups,* pp. 1–12; see especially pp. 6–7.

39. Raymond A. Bauer, "The Obstinate Audience: The Influence Process from the Point of View of Social Communication," *American Psychologist* 19 (1964): 319–28.

40. Eric Berne, *Games People Play* (New York: Grove Press, 1964).

41. Robert R. Carkhuff, *Helping and Human Relations,* Volume 2 (New York: Holt, Rinehart and Winston, 1969), pp. 210–22.

42. Charles B. Truax and Robert R. Carkhuff, *Toward Effective Counseling and Psychotherapy* (Chicago: Aldine, 1967), pp. 163–208.

43. Warren G. Bennis, et al., *Interpersonal Dynamics,* Rev. ed. (Homewood, Illinois: Dorsey Press, 1968), pp. 211–12.

44. Schein and Bennis, *Personal and Organizational Change Through Group Methods,* pp. 41–46.

45. Jack R. Gibb, "The Effects of Human Relations Training," in Allen E. Bergin and Sol L. Garfield (eds.), *Handbook of Psychotherapy and Behavior Change* (New York: Wiley, 1971), pp. 839–62; see especially pp. 840–41.

46. Martin Lakin, *Interpersonal Encounter* (New York: McGraw-Hill, 1972), pp. 7–11.

47. Carl Goldberg, *Encounter: Group Sensitivity Training Experience* (New York: Science House, 1970), pp. 132–35.

48. James V. Clark, "Authentic Interaction and Personal Growth in Sensitivity Training Groups," *Journal of Humanistic Psychology* 3 (1963): 1–13.

49. Frank Friedlander, "The Primacy of Trust as a Facilitator of Further Group Accomplishment," in C. L. Cooper and I. L. Mangham (eds.), *T-Groups: A Survey of Research* (New York: Wiley, 1971), pp. 193–204.

50. Kim Giffin and Bobby R. Patton, "Personal Trust in Human Interaction," in Kim Giffin and Bobby R. Patton (eds.), *Basic Readings in Interpersonal Communication* (New York: Harper and Row, 1971), pp. 375–91.

51. Jack R. Gibb, "Climate for Trust Formation," in Leland P. Bradford, et al. (eds.), *T-Group Theory and Laboratory Method* (New York: Wiley, 1964), pp. 279–309.

52. Fritz Heider, "Perceiving the Other Person," in Renato Tagiuri and Luigi Petrullo (eds.), *Person Perception and Interpersonal Behavior* (Stanford, California: Stanford University Press, 1958), pp. 22–26.

53. Gerard Egan, *Encounter: Group Processes for Interpersonal Growth* (Belmont, Calif.: Brooks/Cole, 1970), pp. 68–103.

54. See Kim Giffin, "The Contribution of Studies of Source Credibility to a Theory of Interpersonal Trust in the Communication Process," *Psychological Bulletin* 68 (1967): 104–20; also Kim Giffin, "Interpersonal Trust in Small Group Communication," *Quarterly Journal of Speech* 53 (1967): 224–34.

55. Jack R. Gibb and Lorraine M. Gibb, "Humanistic Elements in Group Growth," in James F. T. Bugental (ed.), *Challenges of Humanistic Psychology* (New York: McGraw-Hill, 1967), pp. 161–70.

56. Stoller, "A Stage for Trust," pp. 81–96; see especially p. 89.

57. Schein and Bennis, *Personal and Organizational Change,* p. 41.

58. Rogers, "Process of Basic Encounter Groups," pp. 269–72.

59. Fritz Heider, *The Psychology of Interpersonal Relations* (New York: Wiley, 1958), pp. 79–124; see especially pp. 83–122.

60. Edward E. Jones and Keith E. Davis, "From Acts to Disposition: The Attraction

158 Notes

Process in Person Perception," in Berkowitz (ed.), *Advances in Experimental Social Psychology*, Volume 2 (New York: Academic Press, 1965), pp. 219–66.

61. See Harold H. Kelley, "Attribution Theory in Social Psychology," in David Levine (ed.), *Nebraska Symposium on Motivation* (Lincoln: University of Nebraska Press, 1967), pp. 192–238.

62. See M. Duane Thomas, "Developing Human Potential Through Group Interaction" (unpublished doctoral dissertation, The University of Kansas, 1970); and Ronald D. Gordon, "A Quantative Investigation of Selected Dynamics and Outcomes of the Basic Encounter Group" (unpublished doctoral dissertation, The University of Kansas, 1971).

63. See Joseph W. MacDoniels, et al., *Openness: Personalized Expression in Interpersonal Communication*, Research Paper #37 (Lawrence, Kansas: The Communication Research Center, The University of Kansas, 1971; also, Joseph W. MacDoniels, "Factors Related to the Level of Open Expression in Small Group Laboratory Learning Experiences" (unpublished doctoral dissertation, The University of Kansas, 1972), pp. 94–96.

64. Frederick H. Stoller, "Marathon Groups: Toward a Conceptual Model," in Solomon and Berzon (eds.), *New Perspectives on Encounter Groups*, pp. 171–87; see especially pp. 181–85.

65. Sigmond Koch, "The Image of Man Implicit in Encounter Group Theory," *Journal of Humanistic Psychology* 11 (1971): 109–27.

66. Roger Harrison, "Defenses and the Need to Know," *NTL Human Relations Training News* 6, No. 4 (1962): 1–4.

67. Robert R. Carkhuff, *Helping and Human Relations*, Volume 1 (New York: Holt, Rinehart and Winston, 1969), pp. 46–56.

68. Charles A. Kiesler, *The Psychology of Commitment* (New York: Academic Press, 1971), pp. 122–41.

69. Jack R. Gibb, "Defensive Communication," *Journal of Communication* 11 (1961): 141–48.

70. William R. Coulson, *Groups, Gimmicks, and Instant Gurus* (New York: Harper and Row, 1972), pp. 83–95.

71. Morton A. Lieberman, "Behavior and Impact of Leaders," in Solomon and Berzon (eds.), *New Perspectives on Encounter Groups*, pp. 135–70.

72. Kurt W. Back, *Beyond Words* (New York: Russell Sage Foundation, 1972), pp. 213–27.

73. Bertram R. Forer, "Use of Physical Contact," in Solomon and Berzon (eds.), *New Perspectives on Encounter Groups*, pp. 195–210.

74. See Bertram R. Forer, "Therapeutic Relationships in Groups," in Burton (ed.), *Encounter*, pp. 27–41; Coulson, *Groups, Gimmicks, and Instant Gurus*, pp. 53–55; Price M. Cobbs, "Ethno-Therapy in Groups," in Solomon and Berzon (eds.), *New Perspectives on Encounter Groups*, pp. 383–403; see especially pp. 399–401; Richard E. Farson, "Self-Directed Groups, and Community Mental Health," in Solomon and Berzon (eds.), *New Perspectives on Encounter Groups*, pp. 224–32.

75. See Paul Ekman, "Communication Through Nonverbal Behavior: A Source of Information about an Interpersonal Relationship," in Silvan S. Tomkins and Carroll E. Izard (eds.), *Affect, Cognition and Personality* (New York: Springer, 1965), pp. 390–442; Paul Ekman and Wallace V. Friesen, "Head and Body Cues in the Judgment of Emotion: A Reformulation," *Perceptual and Motor Skills* 24 (1967): 711–24.

76. See M. Duane Thomas, "Developing Human Potential," pp. 118–19, and p. 126.

CHAPTER 4

1. William Shutz, *FIRO: A Three-Dimensional Theory of Interpersonal Behavior* (New York: Holt, Rinehart and Winston, 1958), pp. 34–54.

2. Ibid., pp. 54–56.

3. Cf. Jurgen Ruesch and Gregory Bateson, *Communication: The Social Matrix of Psychiatry* (New York: Norton, 1951), pp. 79–81.

4. See David W. Johnson, ed., *Readings in Humanistic Social Psychology* (Philadelphia, Pa.: Lippincott, 1972).

5. Cf. David W. Johnson, *Reaching Out* (Englewood Cliffs, New Jersey: Prentice-Hall, 1972), pp. 9–10.

6. Cf. Schutz, *FIRO,* pp. 22–23.

7. Cf. ibid., pp. 23–24.

8. Ibid., p. 24.

9. Timothy Leary, *Interpersonal Diagnosis of Personality* (New York: Ronald, 1957).

10. Earl S. Schaefer, "A Circumplex Model for Maternal Behavior," *Journal of Abnormal and Social Psychology* 59 (1959): 226–35.

11. Earl S. Schaefer, "Converging Conceptual Models for Maternal Behavior and Child Behavior," in John C. Glidewell (ed.), *Parental Attitudes and Child Behavior* (Springfield, Ill.: Charles E. Thomas, 1961), pp. 124–46.

12. Phillip E. Slater, "Parent Behavior and the Personality of the Child," *Journal of Genetic Psychology* 101 (1962): 53–68.

13. Wesley C. Becker, et al., "Relations of Factors Derived from Parent Interview Ratings to Behavior Problems of Five-Year-Olds," *Child Development* 33 (1962): 509–53.

14. Wesley C. Becker and Robert S. Krug, "A Circumplex Model for Social Behavior in Children," *Child Development* 35 (1964): 371–96.

15. Edgar F. Borgatta, Leonard S. Cottrell, and John M. Mann, "The Spectrum of Individual Interaction Characteristics: An Interdimensional Analysis," *Psychological Reports* 4 (1958): 279–319.

16. Edgar F. Borgatta, "Rankings and Self-Assessments: Some Behavioral Characteristics Replication Studies," *Journal of Social Psychology* 52 (1960): 297–307.

17. See Maurice Lorr and Douglas M. McNair, "An Interpersonal Behavior Circle," *Journal of Abnormal and Social Psychology* 67 (1963): 68–75; Maurice Lorr and Douglas M. McNair, "Expansion of the Interpersonal Behavior Circle," *Journal of Personality and Social Psychology* 2 (1965): 823–30; Maurice Lorr and Douglas M. McNair, "Methods Relating to Evaluation of Therapeutic Outcome," in Louis A. Gottschalk and Alfred H. Auerbach (eds.), *Methods of Research in Psychotherapy* (New York: Appleton-Century-Crofts, 1966), pp. 573–94.

18. Robert C. Carson, *Interaction Concepts of Personality* (Chicago: Aldine, 1969), p. 102. See especially Carson's chapter 4, "Varieties of Interpersonal Behavior," pp. 93–121.

19. Roger Brown, *Social Psychology* (New York: Free Press, 1965), pp. 52, 53. Also see Roger Brown, *Words and Things* (New York: Free Press, 1958).

20. See Robert F. Bales, *Interaction Process Analysis, a Method for the Study of Small Groups* (Reading, Mass.: Addison-Wesley, 1950); and Robert F. Bales, *Personality and Interpersonal Behavior* (New York: Holt, Rinehart and Winston, 1970).

21. See Bales, *Personality and Interpersonal Behavior*, pp. 395–98, 30–50; see especially figures 3.1, 3.2, and 3.3, pp. 33–35.

22. See Erving Goffman, *Relations in Public* (New York: Basic Books, 1971), pp. 194–99.

23. Eric Berne, *Games People Play* (New York: Grove Press, 1964), pp. 91–92.

24. Cf. Leary, *Interpersonal Diagnosis of Personality;* also U. G. Foa, "Convergences in the Analyses of the Structure of Interpersonal Behavior," *Psychological Review* 68 (1961): 341–53; Uriel G. Foa, "Cross-Cultural Similarity and Differences in Interpersonal Behavior," *Journal of Abnormal and Social Psychology* 68 (1965): 517–22; also see Uriel G. Foa, "New Developments in Facet Design and Analysis," *Psychological Review* 72 (1965): 262–74.

25. Cf. Timothy Leary, "The Theory and Measurement Methodology of Interpersonal Communication, *Psychiatry* 18 (1955): 147–61.

26. For a discussion of such tactics and strategies see George R. Bach and Peter Wyden, *The Intimate Enemy* (New York: Morrow, 1968).

27. For a discussion of this principle see Silvano Arieti, *The Will to Be Human* (New York: Quadrangle Press, 1973); see especially chapter 8.

28. See Leary, "Theory and Measurement Methodology," pp. 155–61.

29. For additional empirical support of this principle see Kenneth Heller, Roger A. Myers, and Linda V. Kline, "Interviewer Behavior as a Function of Standardized Client Roles," *Journal of Consulting Psychology* 27 (1963): 117–22.

30. Cf. Erving Goffman, *Behavior in Public Places* (New York: Free Press, 1963), p. 96.

31. See Timothy Leary's discussion of "The Interpersonal Reflex" in Leary, "Theory and Measurement Methodology," pp. 153–56. For a critical evaluation of this contribution by Leary see Carson, *Interaction Concepts of Personality*, pp. 107–15.

32. Leary, "Theory and Measurement Methodology," pp. 152–61.

33. Cf. Carson, *Interaction Concepts of Personality*, pp. 229–32.

34. Cf. Horney's description of the aggressive personality in Karen Horney, *Our Inner Conflicts* (New York: Norton, 1945), pp. 62–72; and Fiedler's studies of leaders who provide very low value ratings of their co-workers in Fred Fiedler, *A Theory of Leadership Effectiveness* (New York: McGraw-Hill, 1967), pp. 44–46 and 49–59.

35. See John W. Thibaut and Harold H. Kelley, *The Social Psychology of Groups* (New York: Wiley, 1959); especially pp. 80–99; George C. Homans, *Social Behavior: Its Elementary Forms* (New York: Harcourt, Brace, 1961). For a summary and evaluation of these two theories see Marvin E. Shaw and Philip R. Costanzo, *Theories of Social Psychology* (New York: McGraw-Hill, 1970), pp. 69–103.

36. Homans, *Social Behavior*, p. 75.

37. Thibaut and Kelley, *Social Psychology of Groups*, p. 21.

CHAPTER 5

1. Chris Argyris, *Interpersonal Competence and Organizational Effectiveness* (Homestead, Illinois: Dorsey Press, 1962).

2. Seymour Feshbach and Roland Singer, "Effects of Fear Arousal and Suppression of Fear upon Social Perception," *Journal of Abnormal and Social Psychology* 55 (1957): 283–88.

3. William V. Haney, *Communication and Organizational Behavior* (Illinois: Richard D. Irwin, 1967), p. 61.

4. Argyris, *Interpersonal Competence,* p. 20.

5. Jean Piaget, *The Psychology of Intelligence* (New York: Harcourt, Brace, 1950), p. 43.

6. Morton Deutsch, "Cooperation and Trust: Some Theoretical Notes," *Nebraska Symposium on Motivation* (Lincoln, Nebraska: University of Nebraska Press, 1962). In Bennis, et al., *Interpersonal Dynamics* (Homestead, Illinois: Dorsey Press, 1964), pp. 576, 578.

7. Erving Goffman, "On Face-Work: An Analysis of Ritual Elements in Social Interaction," *Psychiatry* 18 (1955): 213–31.

8. *Ibid.,* pp. 216, 215.

9. Argyris, *Interpersonal Competence,* p. 18.

10. Jack Gibb, "Defensive Communication," *Journal of Communication* 11 (1961): 143.

11. Carl Rogers, *Client-Centered Therapy* (Boston: Houghton Mifflin, 1951), p. 76.

12. Gibb, "Defensive Communication," p. 144.

13. James E. Dittes, "Attractiveness of Group as Function of Self-Esteem and Acceptance by Group," *Journal of Abnormal Psychology* 59 (1959): 77.

14. Ewart E. Smith, "The Effects of Clear and Unclear Role Expectations on Group Productivity and Defensiveness," *Journal of Abnormal Psychology* 55 (1955): 213.

15. Solomon E. Asch, "Effects of Group Pressure Upon Modification and Distortion of Judgment," *Readings in Social Psychology,* Swanson, Newcomb, Hartley, (eds.), (New York: Holt, Rinehart and Winston, 1952).

16. Bruno Bettelheim. "Individual and Mass Behavior in Extreme Situations," in *Readings in Social Psychology.*

17. B. F. Skinner and Carl Rogers, "Some Issues Concerning the Control of Human Behavior," *Science* 124 (1956): 1057–66.

18. B. F. Skinner, *Walden Two* (New York: Macmillan, 1960), pp. 219–20.

19. Herbert Kelman, "Manipulation of Human Behavior: An Ethical Dilemma for the Social Scientist," in Warren Bennis, Kenneth D. Benne, and Robert Chin (eds.), *The Planning of Change,* 2d ed. (New York: Holt, Rinehart and Winston, 1969).

20. Leonard Krasner, "Behavioral Scientist and Social Responsibility," *Journal of Social Issues* 21 (April 1965).

21. Warren G. Bennis and Herbert A. Shepard, "A Theory of Group Development," *Human Relations* 9, No. 4 (November 1956): 415–37. Reprinted in Robert T. Golembiewski and A. Blumberg (eds.), *Sensitivity Training and the Laboratory Approach* (Itasca, Illinois: Peacock, 1970), p. 93.

22. Ibid.

23. Ibid., pp. 96–97.

24. Ibid., pp. 98–99.

25. Ibid., p. 101.

26. Ibid., p. 107.

27. Ibid., p. 107.

28. Ibid., p. 110.

29. Quotations in this section are taken from Betty Meador, "An Analysis of Process Movement in a Basic Encounter Group" (unpublished Ph.D. dissertation, United State

International University, 1969). Reported in Carl Rogers, *Carl Rogers on Encounter Groups* (New York: Harper and Row, 1970), pp. 121–25.

CHAPTER 6

1. Report in Edgar H. Schein and Warren G. Bennis, *Personal and Organizational Change Through Group Methods: The Laboratory Approach* (New York, Wiley, 1965).

2. Jerome Frank, "Training and Therapy," in Leland P. Bradford, Jack R. Gibb, and Kenneth D. Benne (eds.), *T-Group Theory and Laboratory Method* (New York: Wiley, 1964), pp. 442–51.

3. Kenneth D. Benne, "History of the T-Group in the Laboratory Setting," in Bradford, Gibb, and Benne, *T-Group Theory*, pp. 80–135.

4. Ibid.

5. Ibid.

6. Robert R. Blake and Jane S. Mouton, "The Instrumented Training Laboratory" (Washington, D. C.: National Training Laboratories, NTL Selected Reading Series, No. 5, 1959).

7. Thomas Gordon, *Group-centered Leadership* (Boston: Houghton-Mifflin, 1953).

8. Samuel A. Culbert, "Trainer Self-Disclosure and Member Growth," *Journal of Applied Behavioral Science* 4 (1968): 47–74.

9. Jacob Lomranz, "Discrimination Among Three Types of Trainer Orientations in Sensitivity Training" (unpublished doctoral dissertation, Duke University, 1970).

10. Irvin D. Yalom and Morton A. Lieberman, "A Study of Encounter Group Casualties," *Archives of General Psychiatry* 25 (July 1971): 16–30.

11. Ibid., p. 16.

12. Ibid., p. 28.

13. Ibid., p. 30.

14. Ibid.

CHAPTER 7

1. See Kenneth C. Boulding, *The Image* (Ann Arbor: University of Michigan Press, 1956), pp. 3–5. Cf. George H. Mead, *Mind, Self and Society* (Chicago: University of Chicago Press, 1934), pp. 144–64. Cf. Dean C. Barnlund, "Communication: The Context of Change," in Carl E. Larson and Frank E. X. Dance (eds.), *Perspectives on Communication* (Milwaukee, Wis.: Speech Communication Center, University of Wisconsin, 1968), pp. 24–40; see especially pp. 25–26.

2. For a detailed treatment of this principle see Kim Giffin and Bobby R. Patton, *Fundamentals of Interpersonal Communication* (New York: Harper and Row, 1971), pp. 190–96.

3. Cf. Paul Watzlawick, Janet H. Bevin, and Don D. Jackson, *Pragmatics of Human Communication* (New York: Norton, 1967), pp. 48–54 and 80–93.

4. See Carl Goldberg, *Encounter: Group Sensitivity Training Experience* (New York: Science House, 1970), p. 242.

5. Cf. Roger Harrison and Bernard Lubin, "Personal Style, Group Composition, and

Learning," *Journal of Applied Behavioral Science* 1 (1965): 286–301. Also see Carl Rogers, "The Process of the Basic Encounter Group," in James F. T. Bugental (ed.), *Challenges of Humanistic Psychology* (New York: McGraw-Hill, 1967), pp. 267–76; and Jack R. Gibb, "Meaning of the Small Group Experience," in Lawrence N. Solomon and Betty Berzon (eds.), *New Perspectives on Encounter Groups* (San Francisco: Jossey-Bass, 1972), pp. 1–12; see especially p. 3.

6. See O. J. Harvey, Harold Kelley and Martin M. Shapiro, "Reactions to Unfavorable Evaluations of the Self Made by Other Persons," *Journal of Personality* 25 (1947): 393–411.

7. For a detailed discussion of such problems see Marjorie E. P. Seligman, "Fall into Helplessness," *Psychology Today* 7 (June 1973): 43–48.

8. For a detailed discussion of the process of consideration of potential costs and rewards as they relate to interpersonal relationships see John W. Thibaut and Harold H. Kelley, *The Social Psychology of Groups* (New York: Wiley, 1959), pp. 10–19.

9. Cf. Warren G. Bennis, "Goals and Meta-Goals of Laboratory Training," *Human Relations Training News* 6 (Fall 1962): 1–4.

10. See Carl R. Rogers, *On Becoming a Person* (Boston: Houghton-Mifflin, 1961), pp. 15–27.

11. Cf. Warren G. Bennis, et al. (eds.), *Interpersonal Dynamics*, 3d ed. (Homewood, Ill.: Dorsey Press, 1973), pp. 512–18.

12. Cf. Edgar H. Schein and Warren G. Bennis, *Personal and Organizational Change Through Group Methods* (New York: Wiley, 1965), pp. 28–54; see especially p. 53.

13. See Douglas R. Bunker, "The Effect of Laboratory Education upon Individual Behavior," in Schein and Bennis, *Personal and Organizational Change*, pp. 255–67.

14. Cf. Cary L. Cooper and Iain L. Mangham, *T-Groups: A Survey of Research* (New York: Wiley, 1971), pp. 189–92.

15. For a discussion of this principle and a report on related research, see Harrison and Lubin, "Personal Style," pp. 296–99.

16. Bernard Lubin and Marvin Zuckerman, "Level of Emotional Arousal in Laboratory Training," *Journal of Applied Behavioral Science* 5 (1969): 483–90.

17. See Martin Lakin, *Interpersonal Encounter: Theory and Practice in Sensitivity Training* (New York: McGraw-Hill, 1972), pp. 94–96. Also see Allen T. Dittman, *Interpersonal Messages of Emotion* (New York: Springer, 1972), pp. 87–97.

18. See Phyllis K. Levy, "The Ability to Express and Perceive Vocal Communications of Feeling," in Joel R. Davitz (ed.), *The Communication of Emotional Meaning* (New York: McGraw-Hill, 1964), pp. 43–55. See also Ernest G. Beier, *The Silent Language of Psychotherapy* (Chicago: Aldine, 1966), pp. 55–76. Cf. John Douds, Bernard G. Berenson, Robert R. Carkhuff, and Richard Pierce, "In Search of an Honest Experience: Confrontation in Counseling and Life," in Robert R. Carkhuff and Bernard G. Berenson, *Beyond Counseling and Therapy* (New York: Holt, Rinehart and Winston, 1967), pp. 170–79.

19. See Eric Berne, *Games People Play* (New York: Grove Press, 1964), pp. 13–18.

20. See Michael Beldoch, "Sensitivity to Expression of Emotional Meaning in Three Modes of Communication," in Davitz, *Communication of Emotional Meaning*, pp. 31–42.

21. See Dittman, *Interpersonal Messages of Emotion*, pp. 155–61.

22. Cf. Davitz, *Communication of Emotional Meaning*, pp. 178–87.

23. For a detailed discussion of this principle see Gerard Egan, *Encounter: Group*

Processes for Interpersonal Growth, (Belmont, Calif., Brooks/Cole, 1970), pp. 297–302.

24. See Marvin E. Shaw and Philip R. Costanzo, *Theories of Social Psychology* (New York: McGraw-Hill, 1970), pp. 291–94. Cf. Barnlund, "Communication," pp. 25–26. See also Albert Hastorf and Hadley Cantril, "They Saw a Game: A Case Study," *Journal of Abnormal and Social Psychology* 49 (1954): 129–34.

25. Cf. Schein and Bennis, *Personal and Organizational Change,* pp. 301–7. See Leland P. Bradford, "Membership and the Learning Process," in Leland P. Bradford, Jack R. Gibb, and Kenneth D. Benne (eds.), *T-Group Theory and Laboratory Method* (New York: Wiley, 1964), pp. 190–215; see especially pp. 204–8. Cf. Jack R. Gibb, "Climate for Trust Formation," in Bradford, Gibb, and Benne (eds.), *T-Group Theory,* pp. 279–309; see especially pp. 291–93.

26. Roy M. Whitman, "Psychodynamic Principles Underlying T-Group Processes," in Bradford, Gibb, and Benne (eds.), *T-Group Theory,* pp. 310–55; see especially pp. 319–20.

27. Kenneth D. Benne, Leland P. Bradford and Ronald Lippitt, "The Laboratory Method," in Bradford, Gibb, and Benne (eds.), *T-Group Theory,* pp. 15–44; see especially pp. 25–26.

28. Cf. James V. Clark, "Authentic Interaction and Personal Growth in Sensitivity Training Groups," *Journal of Humanistic Psychology* 3 (1963): 1–13; see especially pp. 2–4. See Matthew B. Miles, "Human Relations Training: Processes and Outcomes," *Journal of Counseling Psychology* 7 (1960): 301–6. Also see Dorothy Stock, "A Survey of Research on T-Groups," in Bradford, Gibb, and Benne (eds.), *T-Group Theory,* pp. 395–441; see especially pp. 430–34.

29. Cf. Frederick H. Stoller, "Use of Videotape Feedback," in Solomon and Berzon (eds.), *New Perspectives on Encounter Groups,* pp. 233–44; see especially 234–38.

30. Cf. J. Douds, et al., "In Search of an Honest Experience," pp. 170–71. Ernest G. Beier, *The Silent Language of Psychotherapy* (Chicago: Aldine, 1966).

31. See James Bebout and Barry Gordon, "The Value of Encounter," in Solomon and Berzon (eds.), *New Perspectives on Encounter Groups,* pp. 83–118; see especially pp. 97–98. Gordon L. Lippit and Leslie E. This, "Leaders for Laboratory Training: Selected Guidelines for Group Trainers Utilizing the Laboratory Method," in Robert T. Golembiewski and Arthur Blumberg (eds.), *Sensitivity Training and the Laboratory Approach* (Itasca, Ill.: Peacock Publishers, 1970), pp. 167–79.

32. For a detailed discussion of problems of accuracy of interpersonal perception see Samuel A. Culbert, "The Interpersonal Process of Self-Disclosure: It Takes Two to See One," in Golembiewski and Blumberg (eds.), *Sensitivity Training,* pp. 73–79.

33. See Richard S. Lazarus and James R. Averill, "Emotion and Cognition: With Special Reference to Anxiety," in Charles D. Spielberger (ed.), *Anxiety: Current Trends in Theory and Research* (New York: Academic Press, 1972), pp. 242–84; see especially pp. 251–53.

34. Cf. John W. Thibaut and Henry W. Riecken, "Some Determinants and Consequences of the Perception of Social Causality," *Journal of Personality* 24 (1955): 113–33.

35. Cf. Dean C. Barnlund (ed.), *Interpersonal Communication: Survey and Studies* (Boston: Houghton-Mifflin, 1968), pp. 151–54. See Howard Leventhal, "Findings and Theory in the Study of Fear Communications," in Leonard Berkowitz (ed.), *Advances in Experimental Social Psychology,* vol. 5 (New York: Academic Press, 1970), pp. 119–86; see especially pp. 139–43.

36. Cf. Gibb, "Climate for Trust Formation," pp. 264–65. See Robert R. Blake, "Studying Group Action," in Bradford, Gibb, and Benne (eds.), *T-Group Theory,* pp. 336–64; see especially p. 343.

37. Jack R. Gibb and Lorraine M. Gibb, "Humanistic Elements in Group Growth," in James F. T. Bugental (ed.), *Challenges of Humanistic Psychology* (New York: McGraw-Hill, 1967), pp. 161–70; see especially pp. 163–65. Frederick H. Stoller, "A Stage for Trust," in Arthur Burton (ed.), *Encounter* (San Francisco: Jossey-Bass, 1970), pp. 81–96. See John Warkentin, "Intensity in Group Encounter," in Burton (ed.), *Encounter*, pp. 162–70.

38. Morton A. Lieberman, Irvin D. Yalom and Matthew B. Miles, "Impact on Partic- ipants," in Solomon and Berzon (eds.), *New Perspectives on Encounter Groups*, pp. 119–34; see especially pp. 131–33.

39. Morton A. Lieberman, "Behavior and Impact of Leaders," in Lawrence N. Solomon and Betty Berzon (eds.), *New Perspectives on Encounter Groups*, pp. 135–71. Also see Lieberman, Yalom, and Miles, "Impact on Participants," pp. 131–33. Also see Irvin D. Yalom and Morton A. Lieberman, "A Study of Encounter Group Casualties," *Archives of General Psychiatry* 25 (1971): 16–30.

40. Lieberman, "Behavior and Impact of Leaders," p. 158.

41. See Kurt W. Back, *Beyond Words* (New York: Robert Sage Foundation, 1972), pp. 153–54; and 213–29. Cf. Robert B. Zajonc, "Cognitive Theories in Social Psy- chology," in Gardner Lindzey and Elliot Aronson (eds.), *Handbook of Social Psy- chology*, vol. 1, 2d ed. (Reading, Mass.: Addison-Wesley, 1968), pp. 320–411; see especially pp. 378–83.

42. See Bertram R. Forer, "Therapeutic Relationships in Groups," in Burton (ed.), *Encounter*, pp. 27–41.

43. Cf. William R. Coulson, *Groups, Gimmicks and Instant Gurus* (New York: Harper and Row, 1972), pp. 87–89. See David W. Johnson, *Reaching Out* (Englewood Cliffs, N.J.: Prentice-Hall, 1972), pp. 9–18.

44. See Frank Friedlander, "The Primacy of Trust as a Facilitator of Further Group Accomplishment," in Cooper and Mangham (eds.), *T-Groups*, pp. 193–204.

45. Robert R. Carkhuff and Bernard G. Berenson, *Beyond Counseling and Therapy* (New York: Holt, Rinehart and Winston, 1967), pp. 173–77. See Gerard Egan (ed.), *Encounter Groups: Basic Readings* (Belmont, Calif.: Brooks/Cole, 1971), pp. 288–89.

46. Cf. Henry Tajfel, "Social and Cultural Factor in Perception," in Lindzey and Aronson (eds.), *Handbook of Social Psychology*, pp. 315–94; see especially pp. 334–38.

47. See David W. Johnson, "The Effects of Expressing Warmth and Anger Upon the Actor and Listener," *Journal of Counseling Psychology* 18 (1971): 571–78

48. See David W. Johnson, "The Effectiveness of Role Reversal: The Actor or the Listener," *Psychological Reports* 28 (1971): 275–82.

49. For a detailed discussion of this principle see Renato Tagiuri, "Person Percep- tion," in Lindzey and Aronson (eds.), *Handbook of Social Psychology*, vol. 3, pp. 394–449.

50. Cf. Charles T. Brown and Charles Van Riper, *Communication in Human Rela- tionships* (Skokie, Ill.: National Textbook Co., 1973), pp. 84–87. See Zajonc, "Cognitive Theories in Social Psychology," pp. 386–88.

51. See Bernard Lubin and Marvin Zuckerman, "Affective and Perceptual Cogni- tive Patterns in Sensitivity Training Groups," *Psychological Reports* 21 (1967): 365– 76. Cf. Richard D. Mann, "The Development of the Member-Trainer Relationship in Self-Analytic Groups," *Human Relations* 19 (1966): 84–117. Also see Brown and Van Riper, *Communication in Human Relationships*, pp. 76–77.

52. Cf. Elliot Aronson, "The Theory of Cognitive Dissonance: A Current Perspec- tive," in Leonard Berkowitz (ed.), *Advances in Experimental Social Psychology*, vol. 4 (New York: Academic Press, 1969), pp. 2–35; see especially pp. 26–30.

53. See Sigmund Koch, "The Image of Man Implicit in Encounter Group Theory," *Journal of Humanistic Psychology* 11 (1971): 109–27. Robert J. House, "T-Group Education and Leadership Effectiveness: A Review of the Empiric Literature and a Critical Evaluation," *Personnel Psychology* 20 (1967): 1–32. Egan, *Encounter Groups*, p. 298.

54. See John P. Campbell and Marvin D. Dunnette, "Effectiveness of T-Group Experiences in Managerial Training and Development," *Psychological Bulletin* 70 (1968): 73–104; see especially pp. 74–75. Cf. Carl R. Rogers and Charles B. Truax, "The Therapeutic Conditions Antecedent to Change: A Theoretical View," in Carl R. Rogers (ed.), *The Therapeutic Relationship and Its Impact* (Madison, Wisc.: University of Wisconsin Press, 1967), pp. 97–108.

55. See Edward E. Jones and Keith E. Davis, "From Acts to Dispositions: The Attribution Process in Person Perception," in Berkowitz (ed.), *Advances in Experimental Social Psychology*, vol. 2 (1965), pp. 219–66; see especially pp. 230–33.

56. Cf. Kenneth L. Dion, Robert S. Baron, and Norman Miller, "Why Do Groups Make Riskier Decisions Than Individuals?" in Berkowitz (ed.), *Advances in Experimental Social Psychology*, vol. 5 (1970), pp. 305–77; see especially pp. 318–24.

57. Cf. Lakin, *Interpersonal Encounter*, pp. 173–78. Cf. Lieberman, "Behavior and Impact of Leaders," pp. 153–55. Schein and Bennis, *Personal and Organizational Change*, pp. 294–99.

58. Lieberman, "Behavior and Impact of Leaders," pp. 153–57.

CHAPTER 8

1. See Jack R. Gibb, "Group Experiences and Human Possibilities," in Herbert A. Otto (ed.), *Human Potentialities* (St. Louis, Mo.: Green, 1968), pp. 41–53.

2. Abraham Maslow, *Toward a Psychology of Being* (New York: Van Nostrand, 1962), pp. 1–8, 97–107, 177–87, 38–39, 188–89.

3. Carl Rogers, *On Becoming a Person* (Boston: Houghton-Mifflin, 1961), pp. 163–96, 39–58. Also see Carl Rogers, *Freedom to Learn* (Columbus, Ohio: Merrill, 1969), pp. 106–12 and 279–97.

4. Erich Fromm, *The Art of Loving* (New York: Harper and Row, 1956), pp. 70–89, 48–52, 6–32.

5. Cf. Suzanne M. Gassner, Jerome Gold, and Alvin M. Snadowsky, "Changes in the Phenomenal Field as a Result of Human Relations Training," *Journal of Psychology* 58 (1964): 32–41. Also Irwin Rubin, "The Reduction of Prejudice Through Laboratory Training," *Journal of Applied Behavioral Science* 3 (1967): 29–50.

6. For a survey of studies on this issue see Cary L. Cooper and Iain L. Mangham, *T-Groups: A Survey of Research* (New York: Wiley-Interscience, 1971), pp. 1–11.

7. For a detailed analysis of personal relationships in a bureaucratic structure see Robert K. Merton, *Social Theory and Social Structure* enlarged edition (Glencoe, Ill.: Free Press, 1957), pp. 249–60.

8. Cf. Chris Argyris, *Interpersonal Competence and Organizational Effectiveness* (Homewood, Ill.: Irwin, 1962), pp. 38–52. See James G. March and Herbert A. Simon, *Organizations* (New York: Wiley, 1958), pp. 22–30.

9. Cf. Leonard R. Sayles and George Strauss, *Human Behavior in Organizations* (Englewood Cliffs, N.J.: Prentice-Hall, 1966), pp. 238–46.

10. Cf. Paul J. Brouwer, "The Power to See Ourselves," *Harvard Business Review* 42 (1964), pp. 156–163.

11. Roger Harrison, "Defenses and the Need to Know," *Human Relations Training News* 6 (1962–1963): 1–4. See Jay M. Jackson, "The Organization and Its Communications Problem," *Advanced Management* 22 (1959): 17–20.

12. Harold J. Leavitt, "Unhuman Organizations," *Harvard Business Review* 40 (1962): 90–98. Warren G. Bennis, "Organizational Developments and the Fate of Bureaucracy," in L. L. Cummings and W. E. Scott, Jr. (eds.), *Readings in Organizational Behavior and Human Performance* (Homewood, Ill.: Irwin, 1969), pp. 434–49. See Lyman W. Porter and Edward E. Lawler, "Properties of Organizational Structure in Relation to Job Attitudes and Job Behavior," *Psychological Bulletin* 64 (1965): 23–51. Cf. Robert C. Day and Robert L. Hamblin, "Some Effects of Close and Punitive Styles of Supervision," *American Journal of Sociology* 69 (1964): 499–510.

13. Cf. Richard H. Hall, "Intraorganizational Structural Variation: Application of the Bureaucratic Model," *Administrative Science Quarterly* 7 (1962): 295–308.

14. Cf. March and Simon, *Organizations*, pp. 109–11.

15. See Sayles and Strauss, *Human Behavior in Organizations*, pp. 249–52, 449–57. Cf. March and Simon, *Organizations*, pp. 67–77.

16. Cf. Chris Argyris, *Integrating the Individual and the Organization* (New York: Wiley, 1964), pp. 6–7. Cf. Bernard M. Bass and Harold J. Leavitt, "Some Experiments in Planning and Operating," *Management Science* 9 (1963): 574–85.

17. Cf. Frank Friedlander, "The Impact of Organizational Training Laboratories upon the Effectiveness and Interaction of Ongoing Work Groups," *Personnel Psychology* 20 (1967): 287–307. Cf. Stephen M. Sales, "Supervisory Style and Productivity: Review and Theory," *Personnel Psychology* 19 (1966): 275–86.

18. Cf. Abraham K. Korman, "Consideration, Initiating Structure, and Organizational Criteria—A Review," *Personnel Psychology* 19 (1966): 349–61. Cf. Michael I. Valiquet, "Individual Change in a Management Development Program," *Journal of Applied Behavioral Science* 4 (1968): 313–25. See John P. Campbell and Marvin D. Dunnette, "Effectiveness of T-Group Experiences in Managerial Training and Development," *Psychological Bulletin* 70 (1968): 73–104.

19. See Dorwin Cartwright, "Achieving Change in People: Some Applications of Group Dynamics Theory," *Human Relations* 4 (1951): 381–92. See Rensis Likert, *The Human Organization: Its Management and Value* (New York: McGraw-Hill, 1967), pp. 167–71.

20. Cf. Warren G. Bennis, "Theory and Method in Applying Behavioral Science to Planned Organizational Change," *Journal of Applied Behavioral Science* 1 (1965): 337–60.

21. Cf. Kenneth D. Benne, "History of the T-Group in the Laboratory Setting," in Leland P. Bradford, Jack R. Gibb, and Kenneth D. Benne (eds.), *T-Group Theory and Laboratory Method* (New York: Wiley, 1964), pp. 80–135.

22. See "What is OD?" *NTL Institute News and Reports* 2 (1968): 1–2.

23. See Robert T. Golembiewski, "Planned Organizational Change: A Major Emphasis in a Behavior Approach to Management," in Robert T. Golembiewski and Arthur Blumberg (eds.), *Sensitivity Training and the Laboratory Approach* (Itasca, Ill.: Peacock, 1970), pp. 361–90. Cf. William B. Eddy, "Management Issues in Organizational Development," in William B. Eddy, et al. (eds.), *Behavioral Science and the Manager's Role* (Washington, D.C.: NTL Learning Resources Corp., 1969), pp. 251–59. Also see Warren G. Bennis, *Organizational Change* (New York: McGraw-Hill, 1966).

24. Cf. Chris Argyris, *Organization and Innovation* (Homewood, Ill.: Irwin, 1965), pp. 2–3.

25. Sheldon Davis, "An Organic Problem-Solving Method of Organizational Change," *Journal of Applied Behavioral Science* 3 (1967): 3–21.

26. For a detailed discussion of this principle see Bobby R. Patton and Kim Giffin, *Problem-Solving Group Interaction* (New York: Harper and Row, 1973).

27. Cf. Warren G. Bennis and Edgar S. Schein, *Personal and Organizational Change Through Group Methods* (New York: Wiley, 1965), pp. 201–33. Cf. Chris Argyris, "Explorations in Consultant-Client Relationships," *Human Organization* 20 (1961): 121–33. See Warren H. Schmidt, "The New Organizational Frontiersman: The Leader-Learner," in Warren H. Schmidt (ed.), *Organizational Frontiers and Human Values* (Belmont, Calif.: Wadsworth, 1970), pp. 21–24.

28. Cf. Warren G. Bennis, *Changing Organizations* (Cambridge, Mass.: M.I.T. Press, 1966), pp. 5–7. First published as a public lecture given at M.I.T.; later reprinted in Warren G. Bennis, Kenneth D. Benne, and Robert Chin (eds.), *The Planning of Change*, 2d ed. (New York: Holt, Rinehart and Winston, 1969), pp. 568–79.

29. See Douglas McGregor, *The Human Side of Enterprise* (New York: McGraw-Hill, 1960).

30. Cf. Warren H. Schmidt, "View at the Frontier," in Schmidt (ed.), *Organizational Frontiers and Human Values*, pp. 3–7.

31. See Eddy, *Behavioral Science and the Manager's Role*, pp. 254–58.

32. Compare these objectives with those discussed by Gilbert Burck, "Union Carbide's Patient Schemers," *Fortune Magazine*, December 1965.

33. Cf. Gordon Lippitt, "Emerging Criteria for Organization Development," *Personnel Administration* 12 (1966). For example of data-collection scales, see Likert, *The Human Organization*, pp. 128–45. Cf. Jay W. Lorsch and Paul Lawrence, "The Diagnosis of Organizational Problems," in Bennis, Benne, and Chin (eds), *The Planning of Change*, pp. 468–78.

34. See Richard Beckhard, "The Confrontation Meeting," *Harvard Business Review* 45 (1967): 149–53.

35. Cf. William B. Eddy, *Behavioral Science and the Manager's Role*, pp. 254–55. Cf. Chris Argyris, "T-Groups for Organizational Effectiveness," *Harvard Business Review* 42 (1964): 174–97.

36. See Kenneth D. Benne, "Some Ethical Problems in Group and Organizational Consultation," *Journal of Social Issues* 15 (1959): 60–67.

37. Cf. Melvin Seeman, "On the Meaning of Alienation," *American Sociological Review* 24 (1959): 783–91. Cf. Simon Marcson (ed.), *Automation, Alienation, and Anomie* (New York: Harper and Row, 1970), pp. 1–2. Cf. William A. Faunce, *Problems of an Industrial Society* (New York: McGraw-Hill, 1968), pp. 100–115.

38. Ben B. Seligman, *Most Notorious Victory: Man in an Age of Automation* (New York: Macmillan, 1966), pp. 211–28. Cf. George Terborgh, *The Automation Hysteria* (Washington, D.C.: Machinery and Allied Products Institute, 1966). See Robert Blanner, *Alienation and Freedom: The Factory Worker and His Industry* (Chicago: University of Chicago Press, 1964), pp. 24–34.

39. Cf. Sigmund Koch, "The Image of Man Implicit in Encounter Group Theory," *Journal of Humanistic Psychology* 11 (1971): 109–27.

40. Cf. Robert Tannenbaum and Sheldon A. Davis, "Values, Man and Organizations," *Industrial Management Review* 10 (1969): 67–83. Cf. B. F. Skinner, *Beyond Freedom and Dignity* (New York: Knopf, 1971), pp. 1–25.

41. Marvin Weisbrod, "What, Not Again! Manage People Better?" *Think,* January–February 1970, pp. 2–9.

42. Cf. Jeremiah J. O'Connell, *Managing Organizational Innovation* (Homewood, Ill.: Irwin, 1968), pp. 125–26.

43. Jack R. Gibb and Lorraine M. Gibb, "Leaderless Groups: Growth-Centered Values, and Potentialities," in Herbert Otto and John Mann (eds.), *Ways of Growth* (New York: Pocket Books, 1971), pp. 107–20.

44. Cf. Carl Rogers, "Foreword," in Lawrence N. Solomon and Betty Berzon (eds.), *New Perspectives on Encounter Groups* (San Francisco: Jossey-Bass, 1972), pp. x–xi.

45. Jack R. Gibb and Lorraine M. Gibb, "Role Freedom in a TORI Group," in Arthur Burton (ed.), *Encounter* (San Francisco: Jossey-Bass, 1969), pp. 42–57.

iNdEx

171

Openness, 12–19, 41–46
Option *not* to change, 131
Organizations, 139–43
Organizational development, 143–46

Perceptions, 11, 13–14, 15, 17–18, 36–40, 41–43, 113–14, 118
Perceptual filters, 120
Personal communication, 11–13, 35–40
Phases in group development, 84–89
Piaget, Jean, 75
Positive reinforcement, 81–82
Power, 80–84
Psychological constraints, 82–83

Relationship dimensions, 54–63, 64–68
Relationship potential, 34–35
Riesman, David, 12
Rogers, Carl, 3–5, 77, 81–82, 97, 136–38
Rokeach, Milton, 12

Schaefer, E. S., 54
Schein, Edgar H., 7–8, 42, 92
Schutz, William, 55, 82
Self-actualization, 137

Self-concept, 20–26, 107–9, 110–11
Self-development, 11–12, 20–26, 111–12, 135
Self-disclosure, 12–13
Shepard, Herbert A., 84–87
Skinner, B. F., 81–82, 97
Slater, Phillip E., 58
Smith, Ewart, 79
Social exchange, 34
Stages of group development, 84–89
Stoller, Frederick, 41
Submission, 57–63, 65–66, 117
Supportive climate, 73–77, 120, 124, 130–31

Task groups, 60
Therapy group leaders, 92–93
Thibaut, John, 34
Thomas, M. Duane, 4
Touching, 49–50
Trainer guidelines, 101–4
Trainer interventions, 100–101
Trainer role, 95–99
Trainer styles, 91–98
Trust, 25–26, 40, 77

Yalom, Irvin D., 98, 99